An Idaho Humanities Council Book

UNIVERSITY OF IDAHO PRESS
Moscow, Idaho

written on water

ESSAYS ON IDAHO RIVERS

Mary Clearman Blew

EDITOR

04 03 02 01 00   5 4 3 2 1

Published 2001 by the University of Idaho Press
Moscow, Idaho 83844-1107
Printed in Canada
All rights reserved.

Library of Congress Cataloging-in-Publication Data
Written on water : essays on Idaho rivers/compiled and edited by Mary Clearman Blew.
   p. cm.
   ISBN 0-89301-224-6 (pbk. : alk. paper)
   1. Rivers—Idaho. 2. Idaho—Description and travel. 3. Landscape—Idaho. 4. Idaho—Biography. 5. Idaho—Social life and customs. I. Blew, Mary Clearman, 1939–

F752.A17 W75 2000
979.6—dc21

                                                          99-058474

Written on Water is the first in a series of imprints made possible in part by the Idaho Humanities Council, the state-based affiliate of the National Endowment for the Humanities. Opinions expressed in the essays do not necessarily reflect the views of either the Idaho Humanities Council or the National Endowment for the Humanities.

The following essays originally appeared in the following publications: "The Clearwater" by Kim Barnes, *River Teeth: A Journal of Nonfiction Narrative* (Fall 1999); "Breathing the Snake" by Claire Davis, *Shenandoah* (Summer 1998); "In the Presence of the Clearwater" by Gary Gildner, *The Georgia Review* (Winter 1998); "The Little Salmon: Confessions at the Edge of the Time Zone" by Joy Passanante, *Weber Studies* (Summer 2000); "What the River Says" by Robert Wrigley, *Five Points* (Fall 1998).

The University of Idaho Press gratefully acknowledges the University of Nebraska Press for granting permission to use "Waiting for Coyote" by Louise Freeman-Toole, to be published in her forthcoming book, *Stand Up to the Rock: Essays on a Snake River Ranch* (2001).

Cover and interior design by A.E. Grey
Cover photo, *Sunset over the Middle Folk of the Salmon*, courtesy of Glenn Oakley.

FOR THE GODPARENTS OF THE IDAHO WRITERS:

Keith & Shirley Browning

Contents

Acknowledgments

Thanks are due to those whose encouragement and hard work have made this anthology possible, particularly to the Idaho Humanities Commission, which provided financial backing; Rick Ardinger, executive director of the Idaho Humanities Commission; the late Margaret Pace, former director of the University of Idaho Press; and Ivar Nelson, current director of the University of Idaho Press, and his staff.

Introduction

On a spring evening in 1997 an audience gathered in the historic old community hall in Moscow, Idaho, to hear several Idaho writers read from their work. I remember the evening as a mild one, trees in bud outside the high, many-paned windows, the light lingering forever, and the contained excitement as more and more people crowded into the wonderful old hall with its wainscoting and hardwood floors, until more and more folding chairs had to be dragged out and set up.

The Latah County Library was sponsoring the evening of readings, and Ron McFarland, who had been assisting the library with a project to bring writers into the community, was the master of ceremonies that night. Buoyant as always, pleased by the large turnout, Ron read a few of his own poems by way of an introduction to the writers who followed: Keith Petersen, Mary Reed, Stephen Lyons, Lance Olsen, Robert Wrigley, Kim Barnes, and me. And as these writers succeeded one another, their voices, their very divergence of insight and experience, their contrasting texts began to converge magically into a rich whole.

In the days following that reading in the Moscow community hall, I began thinking of ways to share the richness of multiple voices with a wider audience. Images of rivers lingered with me (Idaho is

the great state of great rivers), and I thought of the threads of
current, the motion and countermotion, the infinite colors and
tones of water, and the modulations of its music. In assembling an
anthology of original essays about Idaho rivers, I could trust the
writers of Idaho to find harmony in variation.

During the next few weeks, I called writers all over Idaho and
asked them to choose a river. Any river. No, no particular theme,
no set direction, certainly no political agenda. Write an essay in the
direction the river takes you. And the response of the writers was
electric; it was as though everyone I spoke to contained an unwritten
essay on an Idaho river that had waited until now to stir itself.

Readers will find plenty of divergence in this anthology, from
Horace Axtell's and Margo Aragon's evocation of respect for
the water of life in almost-lost, rescued-at-the-brink native values,
to Robert Wrigley's reading of the river as a text, like language
itself, that holds out hope for order and beauty in the chaos
of our days. For some Idaho writers, the river has been a constant
presence in their lives since their eyes first opened on the
sparkle of current, as with Kim Barnes, who struggles to reconcile
vulnerability and courage along the Clearwater, John Rember,
who confronts himself in the mirror of the Middle Fork of the
Salmon, and William Studebaker, who finds consolation for a
vanished past in the rapids of the Snake. For others, the river is a
return from exile: Guy Hand leafs back through memory along
the Boise River, Debra Hieronymus searches for connection in the
shadows of the St. Joe, and Lesa Luders resurrects a lost river
through the story of her father's last canoe trip before the Snake
was dammed. Still others find a new homeplace in rivers: Louise
Freeman-Toole finds her place in the Nez Perce story of Coyote
and the salmon, Gary Gildner plants a garden and cherishes his
small community of neighbors along the South Fork of the
Clearwater, Lance Olsen transplants himself to Bear Creek and is
rewarded by a veritable river of stars.

Of the many themes that run through this collection of essays,
memory and mutability are two of the most prominent. In

"Angling the St. Maries," Ron McFarland remembers the creeks and ditches of a boyhood in Florida; in "The Little Salmon: Confessions at the Edge of the Time Zone," Joy Passanante celebrates the passages of her adulthood as she once celebrated her childhood passages on the Mississippi. Another theme is loss, whether on a personal level, as in the splintering of a marriage in Claire Davis's "Breathing the Snake," or the death of parents and friends in Leslie Leek's "Winter Crossing," or on a more public level, as in Diane Josephy Peavey's concern for her adopted ranching community in "Two Rivers," or Julie Titone's examination of the pollution and subsequent clean-up efforts on the Coeur d'Alene River and the effects on the people who make their home there. But an even more dominant theme is that of strength and renewal, often on a transcendental level, as in William Johnson's "Hiking the Selway at Night." I am reminded of the good fortune of Idaho writers—of all of us who live in Idaho—that we live in a pocket of the earth where we still can touch and smell and see the natural world. We may grieve, we may fear a future where the land will be leveled and the waters tamed and polluted, but we will have hope as long as we are a part of our place. The rivers of Idaho flow to the sea, flow and return, flow and return in the great rhythm of life. May we always cherish their eloquence.

A Drink of Water to All Things

Horace Axtell & Margo Aragon

Horace Axtell, a spiritual leader of the Seven Drum religion and a Nez Perce elder, continues the oral tradition of his people. Margo Aragon, a writer and television producer, interviews Mr. Axtell and transcribes his words into essays that blend oral and written techniques. "A Drink of Water to All Things" is such an essay.

What we call water in Nez Perce, is *kuus*. *Kuus*. And then *yewic kuus* is cold water. That's the way Grandma used to wish, *"Eehax yewic kuus inakuus."* I wish I had a cold drink of water. That's one thing, Nez Perce people have never had a water shortage. I think the important part of water, to the Indian people, is also a place to gain strength. Like the old stories go, our people used to become strong. The power of water was given—power to be strong. Powerful in the sense of, oh, I guess you might say, the vision quests. Every day, early in the morning, a lot of the old warriors used to jump in the cold water and swim. Even if it was icy. This gave them a lot of strength. I guess it was like medicine. It kept them from getting sick, cold. To withstand cold weather. I know a lot of old people who used to do that. They made me do that sometimes. It's a good feeling, though. It's like a recharge, you might say. You feel so refreshed. They used to do that before they ate their morning meal. That's how powerful water is. We all know how important water is to the everyday life of people.

How it is important to the animals, and the plants, and the birds. Just about anything that grows. We know that water is also important to clean our bodies and our faces. Also to prepare our food. This is what we Nez Perce people, a lot of us who believe in the old religion, do: drink water before we eat, to purify our bodies. And then after we eat we drink a little bit of water again to purify the food that we have consumed. This one song I sing a lot is like water you hear. Like the riffles in the water. It's one of the first songs I ever learned in Indian religion. 'Course, we sing our food song and that includes the water, too. All the things that we get from Mother Earth. So, therefore, water has a sacred quality to Indian people.

My grandmother used to go to a certain place where she hadn't been for, maybe, a year. We used to go camping in different areas. When we'd get to a certain place, the first thing, she'd send us down to the spring, or wherever, and get some water so she could drink it. I didn't realize what she was doing, but now I do. It's like a welcome. You feel at home when you drink water from that area. And I know she used to bring water home from different places.

My mother and grandmother used to catch rainwater to water their garden. Get a little dipper and spread water on it. A little bit each day. Also, my mother used rainwater to wash her hair. They say it's very good for hair. So there, again, water comes down from the air, the clouds, and gives a drink of water to all things.

We use water, now, in the modern world, to irrigate fields and to make electricity. Water has been so strong to the importance of people's lives and it seems to me that, at the present time, water has been overused. We're starting to squabble over water. It's getting to the point where people seem to be using water for things to create and make money, which is not what water was put here for. We even have to buy our water now, here, in the cities. That's not the way our old people lived, the Nez Perce people. Water was important in another way. They never used water to make money or anything like that, because it was free. There was no charge to use water, no charge to drink water. It's a blessing to the Nez Perce people. I think most Indian tribes feel that water is very sacred. In a sense where it's a purification each time we drink water. It's a purification of our bodies. Keeps us clean inside. And people don't realize this, how important water is to drink. People nowadays, all of us do, drink water when we take medicine to make that medicine go down into our body. Also, water is regarded like medicine. Because when people get sick, the first thing they give you is a drink of water.

Animals drink water to purify their bodies and eat their food or grass. Then they drink water again. It's a lifestyle for nature. Water is also important to the fish. We call them The Fish People. If it wasn't for water, we would never have any fish. In order to make our fish have an easy way to get up the creeks up here, we must keep our water clean. But nowadays, the water isn't quite like that and neither are the fish, without the proper water. Water holds the number one priority in all life. All people. Without water, nobody would live.

When I lived in the country, we didn't have running water. We had to go get our good water from the spring, almost a quarter mile away. We used to pack water to have drinking water. We had a well about a hundred yards away, but my mother wouldn't let us drink that water. We used to go down to the spring to get our drinking water. It was good cold water. I know we used to have canteens to fill our water, to carry our water to the house. We always seemed to have good clean water.

We're careful with the water we drink. I urge all people to make sure the water is good before they drink too much of it and get sick. It can, in certain times, cause death. As a veteran, I traveled quite a bit of the world. Some places the water was tested by our own personnel and it wasn't fit to drink. It had to be doctored, I guess you might say. They had to put pills in it. I know each time we got a canteen of water we had to put a little iodine pill in there. It didn't taste that great, but it was water. Scientists have done a lot with water. They make good ways to purify water to make it drinkable and useable. You see lots of news in the paper now, where people have to boil their water to drink. And this should be a warning to all people to make sure they test the water and keep it clean for all people. I keep making my children understand how important water is, and not to waste it. Sometimes kids will forget to turn the water off and leave it running. That's just wasting the water.

I used to hear the old people talking about the dams. *'Iweetum,* "blocking off the water," is what they called dams. It's a little different than *falls.* Falls was *'itikem.* So they said *'Iikemhanisiix,* "They are making falls." We used to make little dams to make a little swimming pool for our sweat house or place to bathe. You block the water off and nothing can get by that. It's very hard for anything to go upstream then. So it's like shutting off the water. That's the way all the old people felt about the dams. And this is what happened, too. The fish got cut off and lot of things got cut off, just so there could be electricity and irrigation. I think, maybe, people are beginning to realize what they have done. It's just a thought that I have, myself, because I heard the old people talk that way.

The Clearwater

Kim Barnes

I take the river a step at a time. My feet slide from the shoulders
of rock; my toes wedge between boulders. I am timid about
this, moving out toward center, where the water is deepest, where
the big fish might lie.

Here, at Lenore, the Clearwater is not easy. Too wide to cast from
shore, too swift, too pocked with hidden currents and sudden
holes. I go at it anyway, still without waders, determined to find my
place of stability, the water at my belly, my thighs numbing with
cold.

My husband fishes below me. On shore, our daughter and son dig
pools in the sand, and I feel a rush of gratitude, the joy of living
only minutes from water, the same water I and my brother
played in as children. It is as though I am reliving my own young
life, here on the banks of the Clearwater, as though I exist in two
dimensions and know the pleasure of each—the child's pure
delight in the moment; the woman's recognition of continuance, of
nostalgia, of the water around her and the sun on her face.

I choose a fly I think the fish might favor, its color the color of the
day's light and leaves and wings. I praise its tufts and feathers, its
hackle and tail. I load the line, thinking not of the *S* I must make

through air but of the place above sand where the water eddies, the *V* above whitecaps, the purl below stone.

I do not think of the line or the fly or the fish as much as I think about the water moving against and around me, how the sky fills my eyes and the noise-that-isn't-noise fills my ears—the movement of everything around me like the hum of just-waking or sleep, blood-rush, dream-rush, the darkness coming on, the air.

I forget to watch for the fish to strike, forget to note the catch, the spin, the sinking. I pull the line in, let it loop at my waist, sing it out again, and again. The trout will rise, or they won't. The nubbin of fur and thread will turn to caddis, black ant, stone fly, bee, or it will simply settle on the water and remain a human's fancy. Either way, it's magic to me, and so I stay until my feet are no longer my own but part of the river's bed. How can I move them? How can I feel my way back to shore, where my family is calling that it's time to go home? They are hungry, and the shadows have taken the canyon. They are cold.

From my place in the water, they seem distant to me. I must seem like a fool, numb to my ribcage, no fish to show. But I am here in the river, half-in, half-out, a wader of two worlds. I smile. I wave. I am where nothing can reach me.

☞ ☞ ☞

North Fork, Middle Fork, South Fork, Main: see how the flow of the sounds is smooth, so lovely. The rivers themselves flow together this way, spilling down from the mountains. They drain the north Idaho land my father and others like him logged and loved so easily in the years before their doing so seemed to matter.

Now, as sales are staked and trees are spiked, the land slumps from beneath its covering of burned slash and razored stumps, slides off the hills and down the draws, sloughs off its dying skin like an animal readying itself for another season. Always, the run-off of rain, the soil it carries, the ash and cinder, the dry bones of trees.

Here, where I live with my husband and children above the Main Clearwater at Lenore, twelve miles from where the forks have all come together, we see the movement of land in the water's flow. Spring thaw, and the trees come fully rooted, ungrounded by the wash of high current. Old logjams from previous floods break loose; new ones pile against the bridge footings and small islands. Each becomes a nest of lost things: fishing lures, loops of rope, men's undershirts, women's shoes.

I wonder, sometimes, if my own life's mementos are contained in those tangles, perhaps a barrette I lost while fishing Reeds Creek, or one of my mother's pie tins with which my brother and I panned for gold. Or the trees themselves fallen from the riverbank I sat on as a child, searching for the mussel shells we called angel's wings, though they were mahogany brown and often broken.

What the river takes, the river gives, and so it is with my life here. Each hour I spend with my feet near water, I feel more deeply rooted; the farther I get away, the less sure I am of my place in the world. For each of us, there must be this one thing, and for me it is the river. Not just the river, but the composition that begins as the North Fork and flows into the Main. I have known this river from its feeding waters to its mouth where it meets and becomes one with the Snake. I have known it before the dams, and after. I have known it as a child knows water, have known it as a lover knows water, and now as a mother knows and recognizes water as she watches her own children who are bent at the waist, leaning forward to bring up the sandy wings.

╭ ╭

I am closest to the Clearwater when I am closest to its origins, and to my own. Reeds Creek, Orofino Creek, Weitus Creek, Deer

Creek, the Musselshell—they feed the river as the river feeds me. It has taken me longer to feel intimate with the stretch of river that curves into *omega* below our house. I watch it each day, uneasy with its width and deep holes. I realize, too, that I distrust this length of the river because it no longer moves of its own volition: Dworshak Dam controls a great part of it now. The North Fork, the river I once knew as a tree-lined stream the color of turquoise, now is a man-made reservoir covering over fifty miles of land that was first logged for its timber before being flooded. The river bulges at its base, its narrower neck seemingly unaffected by the distant, concrete obstruction. People drive northeast for hours to reach the Bungalow, Aquarius—places where the water remains swift and the fish are often native.

But I know better. The river's betrayal sometimes shames me, the way it carries on as though what it travels toward is not a state of near stasis, depositing sludge along miles of riprap dikes, piling its dross against the pylons and locks and turbines. It cannot rid itself of what it is given, cannot carry its silt and timber and ash to the mouth of the ocean where it can be broken down, taken to great depths, washed and sifted into sand and dirt. Instead, the silt falls from the slow current, depositing itself in great layers, narrowing the river's channel. The river becomes murky, the flat color of pewter. The trout are replaced by bottom-feeders, lovers of warm water. Every year, the Corps of Engineers sponsors a trash-fish derby, paying the fishermen to catch and kill what their dams have spawned.

Like so many others who love this land, it has taken me some time to understand that this place—its rivers and streams, forests, mountains and high meadows—does not absorb but reflects what we bring to it. Perhaps, then, what I see in the river is some mirror of the contradictions that make up my own life—the calm surface, the seeming freedom. Certainly, the river is a metaphor for memory. "I am everything I ever was," Stegner wrote, and so it is with the river—water and rock, metal and mineral, stick and bone, trout-flash and deer-lick. Perpetual, even in the face of destruction, I think, even as I read the sad stories of pollution and poisoning, fish-kill and disease. Perpetual because the rain must fall and the mountains must accept and the water must run toward ocean. A comfort, knowing that the amount of water in our world never changes, that there is never any more nor any less, only the same and in various forms: ice, liquid, steam. I trust that water will withstand, given its basic demands—to fall, to move, to rise, to fall again.

This, then, may be my final recognition: the inevitability of movement. We slow, we go forward. We age. We rise to greet each morning. We fall into sleep each night. Constant as rain, perpetuated in death and birth and rebirth.

It has taken me time to understand the need I feel to be consumed by the river. Raised a stoic, I am seldom given to need. Need is a weakness, a loss of control, the Achilles heel of human existence. My connection to the river is complicated by its pull; I resent the power it possesses to draw me. Yet I want its sound in my ears, its smell, its taste. I want to be immersed—my hands, my feet, my hips. Like all seductions, it necessitates surrender.

I am learning to let go.

⌒ ⌒ ⌒

I bring to the river my love and those that I choose to love. I bring to it my child's memories and my woman's life. I bring to it hunger but always joy, for whatever it is that weighs on me dissipates in those few miles between our house in the canyon and the water's edge.

I understand how water can become something grim, how it can rise and take and swirl and drown. How it can become something to fight against, something to resist. The dam on the North Fork, the largest of its kind, was not built for electricity or simple recreation, they say, but for flood control in Portland, four hundred miles west.

There's less flooding now, although three springs ago, in 1996, not even the dams could keep pace when the temperatures rose and the snow-melt came down with rain. We watched from our house above the river, stranded between washed-out roads, watched the roofs and porches, the dead cows and refrigerators and lawn chairs, the still-intact trailer house that slammed against the Lenore Bridge.

How can I cheer such destruction? For that is what I felt, an overwhelming sense of boosterism. I wanted the river to win in some essential way, wanted to see it rise up and lash out, pull down the dams and drain the reservoirs, ferry away the docks and cleanse itself of silt. I wanted it to show a god's righteous anger, a larger reflection of my own frustration and resentment.

I didn't mind, then, that we couldn't get out. My husband had made a last, grand effort to snatch our children from their school in Orofino twenty miles east, hauling them back over bench roads not yet torn away by the massive run-off, roads that crumbled and disappeared behind them. Other rural parents with children in school were not so lucky: it would be a week before any travel was allowed in or out, except by helicopter. Our family was together, protected by our place high on the canyon wall. We had food, water, wood. We had days ahead of us without school or teaching, weeks before the roads would be cleared, and now the sun that had started the ruin was back out and warming the air into spring.

We packed sandwiches and cookies, cheese and crackers and a bottle of fine red wine. We hiked to where we could watch Big Eddy, the place where the river curled against itself and created an enormous back current that caught and held the debris. While the river ran thick with trees and fence posts, goat huts and wall-papered sheeting, we ate and drank and gathered ladybugs for our garden. Certain logs were red with their hatching, their coming out of hibernation. We scooped them up in handfuls and carried them in bundles made of paper towels and candy wrappers. Their odor was strong, dry, astringent—a promise of summer.

We watched a jetboat make its way down the river. Foolish, we thought, to risk such danger. The river was running at a near-record high; the water was choked with flotsam, some larger than the boat itself. The two men inside were not wearing life jackets, and I shook my head. What were they thinking?

The boat pulled in at a smaller eddy downstream, and there we saw what they followed: a large raft of finished lumber, floated loose from the mill at Orofino. Scavengers' rights. If they were willing to risk it, the lumber was theirs.

One man kept the helm while the other bent over the gunnels to grab the wood. They pulled it onto the boat's bow one plank at a time until the craft sat low in the already threatening water. We held our breath, knowing that if they were to fall overboard or if the boat capsized, we could do nothing but watch.

They loaded the wood. They let the current swing them about, turn them upstream. They made their way slowly, navigating through tangles of barbed wire still stapled to barn doors, past trees three times the length of their boat. They had their booty. They were gone.

I couldn't imagine such nonsense, such greed. What desperation could bring on the willingness to risk so much for so little? I felt content, driven by nothing other than the warmth on my shoulders and the love I felt for this land and my husband and daughter and son, who gathered around me to show what they had found: a mantid's egg case, triangular and strangely textured, like meringue hardened and fired to a ceramic glaze. We would take it home as well and put it in the garden, where it would hatch its eaters of grasshoppers and aphids.

I must have believed, then, that it was love that would see me through the long hours of darkness, that would keep me grounded during the wild summer heat. I must have believed, like the river, what we love may surge and wane but remains nonetheless constant, giving, taking, carrying on.

And doesn't it? Perhaps it is we who fail love, refusing to allow its seduction, its pull and sway. Love is a river we step into, like the waters of baptismal rebirth. We close our eyes. We bow our heads. We allow ourselves to be taken as the water closes over our heads. For that moment, we must believe.

⌒ ⌒ ⌒

"I don't think we can make it." I looked at what was left of the road, stretching down before me into a dusk of low trees.

My daughter and son moaned. After a day of writing, I had picked them up from the sitter's in Orofino, promising a late afternoon along the river. My husband was in the mountains near McCall, hiking the upper lakes, safe with the friends he'd known since high school. There was a place I'd heard of, just down some side road, where Ford's Creek met the river, a place with sand and stiller water, where Jordan and Jace could swim and I could spread my blanket and think. The stretch of river we were after mattered to me: it was a section of the last few miles of the Main Clearwater, the last free-flowing water between the headwaters and the ocean.

I needed the river in a way I had not only hours before. It wasn't fishing I was after. I was sour with bad news, begrudging even the rod, line and fly their pacification. That afternoon, I'd gotten a phone call from across the country and learned that our close friends' marriage was in sudden and serious peril, rocked by confession of a particularly insidious spate of infidelity. The levels of betrayal had shocked me, and the narrative of contentment and ongoing friendship that I had trusted was suddenly gone.

The anger that I felt surprised me. I am not comfortable with anger, having been taught from the cradle that anger, like other unmanageable emotions, is best kept under lock and key, somewhere in the heart's deepest chamber. The river would help, sweep away the confusion of emotions with its own ordered chaos. The river would help me find my footing, my point of rest.

But now this: I'd chosen the wrong road. Even after having made the decision to put the car into reverse and back our way out of the ravine, we were going nowhere. The tires of the front-wheel-drive Toyota spun and chattered in the gravel, unable to push the weight of the car up such a steep incline. The dirt and basalt-studded bank rose close on my left; the road crumbled away on my right, slumping into a gully of black locust, poison ivy, and blackberry brambles thick with thorns.

"*Now* what." I said it in the way my mother always had. Fatalism. Tired resignation.

I eased the clutch, tried again. Nothing but smoke and the bitter smell of burning rubber.

"I think we'd better get out of the car," Jace said. At seven, he's the cautious one, always sensing the adult's boundless capacity for error.

"No," I said. "It's okay. Let's just go on down. We can turn around at the bottom." I had no idea if this were true, but my choice was to keep going or for us all to begin the long walk back to town for a tow truck. I also felt a kind of apathy: what was the worst that could happen? The river was only five hundred yards away. We'd find our way out.

What we found instead was an increasingly narrow once-road. I saw that, for years, the rain had washed down the path scraped from the hillside, taking what dirt remained with it to the river. What was left was a deep schism that forked and meandered its way around rocks too large to be moved. I concentrated on riding the ruts' shoulders until there was no rut to straddle but only a series of woven ditches. I kept thinking it would get better, that the road would even out, that *someone* had made it down here because the vegetation was scraped from the center. I kept wishing for the Suburban with its high clearance and granny-gear, but I doubted that the path we traveled would have allowed its girth.

We bounced over boulders the size of basketballs. The skidplate caught and dragged. Jordan and Jace whimpered in the backseat. I tried to act as though this were nearly normal, to be expected. If I stayed calm, in control, they would feel safe.

"Mom, please." Jordan had her hand on the door handle, as though she meant to jump.

"We're almost there," I said. "We'll get to the river and be glad."

We were far into the darkness of trees now, the yellow pine and locust, the dense undergrowth of vine maple. I jostled the car around a corner, then stopped. I could see ahead to where the road leveled off, where sunlight broke through. Between us and that point of flat ground was a final pitch downward, where the road hooked a ninety-degree angle. The bigger problem was that the trail became narrower still, hedged in by the bank on the left and, on the right, by an old tanker truck settled into a bog of brambles.

I examined my passage. A boulder twice the size of our car protruded like a tumor from the eight-foot dirt bank. The abandoned tanker, its red paint faded to rust, was just as intractable: steel and stone, and only the space of a small car between them.

If I stop here, I thought, the tow truck might still be able to reach us. But I had begun to doubt the plausibility of such a rescue, given the tight turns and narrow corridor down which we had traveled. I thought cable, winch, but could not imagine the logistics of being dragged backwards from the ravine without damaging the car beyond repair.

"Mom?" My son's voice quavered.

"What?" I was snappish, weighing our chances, calculating the risk.

"Can't we just walk from here?"

I thought of the brambles, the probability of rattlesnakes, what unseen dangers might wait around the corner.

"Just hang on." I inched the car toward the passage, like Odysseus steering his ship through the straits. I sucked in and held my breath, giving the air what room I could. One scrape and we were through and bumping into the clearing.

Whoops and hollers from the backseat. "We made it!" Jace shouted. Jordan crowed. I stopped the car, got out and circled it twice, looking for damage. Nothing but a few shallow scratches. No dripping oil. The muffler remained miraculously intact.

"Watch for snakes. Wait for me." I gathered our water bottles and bag of sandwiches, taking in the lay of the land. Between us and the river was the railroad track, built high on its ridge of rock. To the left, I saw the remnants of a gold mine, its entryway framed in old timbers. To my right was a settling pond, green with algae. As we began our short walk, two blue herons rose from the still water, awkward on their wings.

There was a game trail, which we followed to the tracks and over. What we found was a long beach of rocks and a smaller one of sand. The children had all but forgotten the trauma of our trip and stripped themselves of shoes and socks before wading in. I felt the heat, then, the sweat gone sticky at my collar and waist.

I walked a few yards upstream, found a rock close to water, where I could dangle my feet and keep an eye on my son and daughter. I tried not to think of the sun's low slant, the hard way out. I tried not to hear what I was thinking: there *is* no way out of here except to leave the car and walk. No way I could make that first climb and twist between the rock and truck.

I closed my eyes. The river filled my ears, and I began to float with the sound. I needed to find something to dislodge the fear— not only of the trek ahead of us, but the fear that had come while listening to my friend's grieving. It could happen, any time, any place, to anyone. One minute, you're on solid ground, the next moment the earth has cracked open beneath you. You get up in the morning and look in the mirror and tell yourself what the day will consist of, and then the light jerks sideways and you are left falling through the dark.

Behind me, a dog barked. I turned to see a large yellow lab, and then an older man walking the tracks. He stopped and raised his hand in acknowledgment of our presence. I hesitated, suddenly aware of another danger: a woman, two children, alone.

He could help us, I thought. He might live close by, have a tractor or winch. I thought, I can't let him know we're stuck here, can't let him see how vulnerable we are.

"How's it going?" he yelled.

I nodded and gave him a thumb's up. He stood for a long time, and I thought he might decide to walk toward us. And then what? For all I knew, he was one of my father's old logging friends. For all I knew, he was a transient bent on some evil.

He stayed on the track, and I watched him disappear around the bend. There was too much to be afraid of, too much to fear. I rose and waded the rocks toward my children, suddenly distrusting even the river, its currents here strange and unpredictable.

They were making a catch basin for the small minnows they caught in the net of their hands. They hardly noticed my presence. I should have them gather their things, I thought, hustle them toward the car, or herd them in front of me up the rag of road, where we could walk the asphalt into town. It would take hours, I knew, hours into dusk, a woman and two children on a rural road where few cars traveled after dinner. I could hear my mother's scolding voice, the one I have known all my life, consistent through all my unwomanly adventures and forays: "What in the world were you thinking? What could have made you take such a risk?"

Risk. I looked across the river, where Highway 12 tied east to west. Cars flicked through the trees, distant and quick. I knew the benefits of being where I was: the water comforted me, the sand and rock and cottonwood leaves turning golden in the last rays of sun. I needed this, often and sometimes desperately. I believed, too, that my children were made better by such a landscape, that every handful of water they dipped from the river was an hour they would later remember as good.

But why here? Why hadn't I been content to take the easy way, pull off the road and find the familiar beaches and banks, Pink House Hole or Big Eddy, Myrtle or Home Beach?

I looked up, then down the far bank. This part of the Clearwater was different from farther downriver. Not so big. The rocks on the other side seemed still part of the canyon wall, huge and jagged from the blasts of road-making. Maybe it was good to be in a place I had not memorized, to be surprised by stone and current. I ran my hand through the water, patted the back of my neck. I needed to remember what I believed in, remember that things might just as easily go good as bad.

I called my children in. They refused to be hurried, reluctant as I to face the trip out, though it would be much easier, I had cozily assured them, going up than down.

Mosquitoes clouded around us as we walked from the river toward the pond. My daughter swatted frantically: they are drawn to her especially, and their bites leave her swollen and miserable.

"Hurry," I said. "It's getting dark. We need to get out while there's still light."

We crowded in, full of sand and river smells. I made a last check of the ground beneath the car: no oil or other inappropriate leakage. We made a tight turn, and I sighed as we faced the hill. What was it worth to attempt the ascent, lose the muffler, bash in the doors? We wouldn't be killed. What were my choices? It seemed an impossible decision.

I thought of the mosquitoes, the long walk out with two tired children, our feet rubbed raw by wet shoes and sand. I said, "Buckle your seatbelts and lock your doors." I gave the engine more gas than usual.

The first pitch was not dirt and rock but a slick of muddy clay beneath a thick layer of pine needles. We spun, then began sliding backwards, back into the long thorns of locust, over boulders and humps because the car could not be steered in such muck.

When we came to a stop, I leaned forward, rested my forehead against the wheel. I thought I might cry.

"Mom?" My son's voice was high, nearly shrill.

"Yes, Jace."

"I'm out of here."

He opened his door before I could stop him, slammed it shut and ran for the railroad tracks. Jordan was fast behind.

I rolled down my window. "Okay," I said. "You stay right there, this side of the tracks. Don't you move. If I can get past this first pitch, we'll make it. When you hear me honk, come running." They nodded, miserable among the mosquitoes, shaking in the suddenly cool air.

I backed up as far as I could, put the car in first, gunned the engine and popped the clutch. I hit the hill with my tires screaming, went up, careened sideways, bounced off the boulder, lost traction and stalled, then slid all the way back down, cringing with the screech of metal against rock, wood against metal.

I need to focus on the initial few yards instead of the dog-leg corner at its summit, I thought—the boulder bulging from the hillside, the tanker truck with its sharp edges. If things went well, we could get out with minimal damage. If things went badly, I might slide down into the gully with the truck, be swallowed by blackberries, have to fight my way out of thorns and lord knew what else.

I got out of the car, tried to pull some of the larger rocks off the road, broke off what branches I could. I scuffed at the pine needles, realizing the uselessness of it: the ground underneath was saturated with moisture. I backed up, got a stronger run. Black smoke clouded around me. I got a foot farther before sliding back down.

I went at it hard then, again and again, as the sun settled lower in the west and the sky darkened. I was still afraid, still fearing too much power, too much speed. It was best to keep control, stay steady. But I got no farther. Always, almost to the top, and then the sudden spin and slide.

How many times? Twenty? Thirty? I didn't care about the car anymore, hardly heard the worried cries of my children. I was feeling something building inside of me, something I hadn't felt for a long time. It was hard and headlong, heedless in a way that might be brave. I'd felt it often before, when I was younger and wildly free. No husband. No children. Only my own life in my hands. I'd felt little fear of anything then, and it was a comfort. Now, with so much to love and lose, I'd come to cherish the expected, the easy ways. Risk came in larger increments: sickness, infidelity, divorce, death. I'd begun to live my life as though, by giving up the smaller risks, I could somehow balance out the larger, keep the big ones at bay with a juju bargain—the sacrifice of whatever independence and strength such risks brought me.

Sitting there, the car smelling of rubber and smoke, the heat and the mosquitoes and darkness coming on, I felt something else, and it was anger. Anger at what I feared and must fear, anger that I was where I was and in possible danger.

I felt suddenly and awfully alone, not because of the isolation, but because I was a woman where I should not be, having risked too much for the river.

The car idled. I hit the dash with the heel of my hand. I let all of it come into me, then—the anger I felt at love and death, at men who might hurt me and the men who would never, at the car and the land in its obstinacy. I felt the quiver in my belly and the rush of heat that filled my ears. I needed speed, momentum to carry me though.

I revved the engine, popped the clutch. I made the turn and didn't slow down. I kept it floored. I hit the boulder, jerked the wheel hard to the left, hit the truck. The tires spun. I didn't know what was behind me now, what I might slide into. I turned the wheel this way, then that, seeking purchase. I yelled at the top of my lungs, "You son-of-a-bitch, go!" And then I was up that first pitch and breathing.

The kids came running, screaming, shouting. They piled gleefully into the car. We were going to make it. Everything was okay.

But it wasn't, because now there was another pitch, and then another. We spun. We stalled.

They got out. They ran all the way back to the railroad tracks.

I rocked the car back against the tanker. Bounce, spin, back. Bounce, spin, back. Each time a little farther, and when I found my ground and started careening up, I didn't stop. I bounced the car out of the canyon, figuring the exhaust system was already gone, figuring it had all been decided hours ago and this was the final scene.

When I got to the highway, I set the emergency brake and jogged back down. Jace and Jordan were coming to meet me, exhausted and still frightened. I batted at the mosquitoes and hurried us all up the hill. I was laughing, giddy with adrenaline. They were weepy, a little confused by my gaiety. They never wanted to do it again.

"It was an adventure," I told them. "And see? We're fine."

As we drove the highway home, I felt vibrant, exhilarated. The moon rising was the most beautiful thing, the wind through the windows a gift. I'd check the car for damage tomorrow, but for now nothing could touch us.

My children would sleep well, and I knew that in years to come, they would tell this story and the story would change and remain the same. Always, there would be the road we traveled, the rocks, the ruts, the mine to the east, the tanker to the west. There would be the night and mosquitoes, the smoke as they watched the car beat its way out of the canyon. There would be their mother's foolishness or her bravery, her stubborn refusals. The words might change, and maybe their fear. But always, there would be the river. It would run cold and loud beside them, the water they cupped in their hands and held above the sand to be sieved and rained and cupped again.

It will keep them near me. It will carry them away.

Breathing the Snake

Claire Davis

The river rocks me. Lifts me until my feet hang plumb from my body, lowers me between swells, heel and toe touching sandy bottom. I've biked the thirty miles from home. I know this stretch well enough to ride it blind, and it seems I have—for I don't remember the ride or the road. I've left the bike at the top of the cliff at my back, dropped it in the roadside gravel, walked out into this river clothed and intentional. The stepped hills across the way were fired last night, by lightning, and though by chance, in the height of the storm, I'd actually seen the distant smoke, at this moment, with the scorch still stinking and the charred slopes black against the blue sky, I don't see it. I've come to a place in my life that I thought I'd never see. I am middle-aged and having waded my way out of the debris of a reckless youth and a failed first marriage, I'd come finally, again, to believe in myself, in the orderliness of work, in the solace and passion of a good marriage. And even though in summer this valley wilts at the mouth of Hells Canyon like the opening of a brick oven and the high desert rims one side of it encouraging prickly pear, puncture weed, rattlesnakes and drought, I believed most in the kindnesses. I believed that the basalt hills would shelter me as they did this valley, and this valley with its river dammed to slackwater, its clement winters encouraging a luxury of dogwood and roses, wisteria and grape, its forgiving fall after the hot, dry summer, would encourage this same accommodating grace in the willfulness of my own heart. I believed my life good, my course set. But in the span of an afternoon, it has all disappeared. All I see is the river, wide and fast and true—that thing to which I have come, to trust with my life.

It is the Snake River, flowing out of Hells Canyon—deepest gorge in the country—and this part of the river marks the boundaries of western Idaho from eastern Oregon and Washington. For two years now, summer, spring and fall, I have been biking a small stretch of this river. From my home in Lewiston, Idaho, I cross the river into Washington and upriver to Buffalo Eddy, about forty miles one way. Although I bike almost daily, it is not always the full distance—depending on time and weather—but it is always this route, this river.

I don't know rivers. They're not in my nature. I am a Wisconsinite where water mostly stands still—lakes, sloughs, wetlands. Rich, rich in water. We used to joke about Minnesota, "land of ten thousand lakes," how poor, to be able to count the number of lakes. I am still new to the West, a short ten years, and even newer to Idaho. The larger, riverless part of my life, thirty-seven years, I lived within a twenty-five-mile radius of the place where I was born—farmlands tuck-pointed in fences. My parents, brother and sister, aunts, uncles and cousins still occupy that rooted sphere.

Out here water rushes away, propelled down slopes in freshets and avalanches, pours off the face of the land in harrowing channels, forms and reforms the earth, a series of changes that frankly terrifies me. So much inconstancy.

I am buoyed by the river, lifting and falling, following the current with my eyes, how it snags the spit of land in the near distance, diamond chop that for once fails to glitter. I cannot begin to think of how my life has become a sustained wreck, how I want to go back to the early morning and wake to a different day, a different landscape. Or not wake. The current is a broad stroke away. I can feel its pull, but my body is strong, as I'd fought to make it these past two years, and I hold my ground even as it's shifting from under my feet.

☞ ☞ ☞

The first time I bike along the Snake it's two years earlier, summer. Biking is an old love I take up again to shed these middle years' indulgence, the writer's sedentary days and nights, my concession to the fusing bones in my feet. It's a capitulation of will to age and appetite that has taken place over a period of five years, giving in, giving out. Up until recently I was still smoking three packs a day. Even walking had become a chore—breathless on stairs, I'd get to the top and light up. This is age I'd say. But now I'm pushed out of myself, out of my house by some deeper urge.

This was a spring of flooding. A one hundred years' flood and all the dikes, dams, levees and spillways couldn't keep the waters back. Although amid the destruction—roads blown out, towns abandoned to the National Guard, houses submerged or unmoored to float down the spring tide—Lewiston was spared, an island in a national disaster zone. By now, the worst of the floods are long done, but the effects are still visible. The Snake River is brawling and muddy. I bike the levee and the river is uncomfortably close with its cargo of logs and boards, spin drift and the occasional carcass—a deer with its rack shimmied into the branches of a tree. Renegade logs stack in colliding rafts against the Memorial Bridge, grind a curious complaint under water and work their way loose to float down the confluence of the Snake and Clearwater on down to the Columbia, ocean bound.

I keep to the levee and its safe asphalt path, though parts have been closed off because they're still under water, and I stop a cautious distance above the blockades. The surface foams and bubbles like a pot set on simmer. It's a sticky brew that stinks of high timber and snow, pulp wood, fish, the first vegetation, and mud.

The surrounding hills are a clean green and I spend a better part of that first month with my eyes raised to them. I avoid looking at the water. God only knows what might come boiling down the current. There's always the car wreck, the capsized boat, the drunken man who stumbled away from his friend's wedding. There's always a body in the river, some gone to pieces over years and under logs. It's in the relentless nature of big waters, to subsume whatever the landscape offers itself, be that canyon rock or careless people, suck them under, wear them down to gravel and sand, pitch it all up in midchannel spits, or sandy beaches. It's a deeply black view I have of this river with its grinding hydraulics, its hidden currents, its lore of the dead. An untrustworthy thing, a thing I cannot look at head on, but must keep in my peripheral vision, as if it might change course midday, midride, and sweep me over the levee rocks, as if it might rise in a tidal wave and take me, along with this entire valley.

I grow stronger, and bored. By late summer the levee has lost its challenge, the treeless hills are burnished brown and the rows and stacks of houses nesting the cliffs shimmer in waves of heat, bake to bleached colors. Here is the Clarkston Heights subdivision, over there the Elks' cement-and-glass bunkered clubhouse. Here a subdivision, there a subdivision. Hells Gate State Park with its RV caravans and chained poodles. The river has dropped, and the center, where it holds the sky, has turned a clear blue. The valley temperature hovers in the nineties. I've gained muscle in these daily rides, regained my wind. I pedal the entire levee there and back and back again. More than ever I'm restless, on the road and at home. My husband, Dennis, dislikes biking, can't understand my compulsion.

It is an early afternoon, and I am on the back porch, unchaining the bike. Dennis leans against a pillar. His blond hair sticks up in quills under the nervous combing of his fingers. His careful distance seems almost natural now. And when did that happen? I can tell he wants to say something, but hesitates and this too is new, this awkwardness. When I thump the bicycle down the steps he follows. I feel chased and stop in the yard, turn to him.

"You're not riding this bike for the same reason as in Mukwonago, are you?" he asks. He ducks his head, his neck exposed—how white his skin is, how nearly translucent with light. We both know what he means. The last time I took to the bike was just before I separated from my first husband, when I lived in Mukwonago, Wisconsin. He was a big man, six foot two to my five foot three. I was getting strong, riding thirty to forty miles a day. Readying myself for battle.

I laugh, is that all? "Of course not," I say, and I believe I mean it. "I'm just getting fit," and this is true, the old me, the body I am most acquainted with is reemerging; thirty pounds lighter, I begin to recognize myself when I catch glimpses in store-front windows. I reach over and brush his arm, feel the tightness in the muscle under my palm. I say, "The novel's in New York and I can't sit still," and this too is true. When I ride away, it's with a light heart. I tell myself it's because his worries are unfounded. I tell myself it's because I'm reassured he still loves me. I tell myself I still love him. We are, I believe, who we have always been.

It's Hells Canyon that I aim for—that sketchy gap in the distant hills. Dennis and I have driven up it a couple times in the truck. A narrow, twisting, ill-bred little road that's dangerous at the best of times, even in a vehicle. I'd ooh and aah, plant my feet on the dash and sweat against the vinyl seat until we'd come to Buffalo Eddy where we'd get out to look at the petroglyphs roadside. Then my husband would turn the truck for home and I'd feel this immense relief to be out of the constriction of basalt walls.

And now here I am biking out of Asotin, with the towns and ranches falling behind me, heading out on a road that's hardly safe for biking, up a canyon that by midday will be a slow cooker, and I'm level with the river for the most part, a short hop away from the water, eye to eye with that thing I've avoided.

The Snake.

This is not the slackwater I have become cozy with—that deeply pooled backwater with its swimming beaches and teenage angst beating out of boom boxes, coveys of jet skis, wild Canada geese turned domestic, rock chucks grown fat on Danish and sweet rolls. This stretch above Asotin is the Snake still fresh from Hells

Canyon's steep walled gorges, with rapids and riffles, drops and eddies. I bike close to the cut banks, the eroding islands, the miles of rocks piled high and dry—the clutter of floods. *This* river is a winnowy thing, slippery in its casual destruction, its lack of intent. I head for Buffalo Eddy, an ambitious ride, and I keep my eyes raised to the hills soaring above, hosts to the swallows' nests—mud wallows abandoned to the heat of the season—the cliff-side spiders—great fleshy dollops in a crosshatch of webs—and the columnar basalt outcroppings—home to bighorn sheep.

On bike, I insert myself into this landscape. I pause to study and explore. I drift, alternately mindless and aware. I meditate. I breathe it. I take it into my body. The sun blisters the back of my neck and the tops of my legs. I push on. At Buffalo Eddy I let out a whoop and scale the rocks down to the river. I find a shallow pool and step in up to my knees, ladle water over my breasts and back, face and neck. The river is a white noise beneath the grousing of magpies, the heckling jays. Back on shore I stretch out on basalt, look up the canyon, always up to where the sky collides with the cresting hills. In a contest of wills between river and land, I say, *Do your worst, river. The hills will always be here.* What I do not know is that over the course of this next year the river will cut a channel as deep in me and as irrevocable as it has the canyon.

⌒ ⌒ ⌒

The old river captains argue about whether the river is 130 feet deep or bottomless at Buffalo Eddy. It's a narrow squeeze between basalt outcroppings, and the score of whirlpools on the river's surface are just a suggestion of the turmoil beneath. It's said that at times, at this point in the river, and for unexplainable reasons, it rises like a person lifting from his seat, up and up and over the rocks with a great roar of rushing water. I've never witnessed this. It's one of a multitude of stories about this spot. I've no doubt this portion of the Snake is one of the more dangerous. Before the river was dammed, when it was still in its wildest youth, whole logs were scooped into whirlpools, and upended, churned like wooden spoons in batter before being sucked from sight. The occasional boat went the same fatal route. A quarter mile down river some of them resurfaced with a boom, others are said to still be down there, stirring, endlessly stirring. Even now, people navigate this channel warily. White crosses mark spots where unfortunate swimmers found the current.

It is spring, my second year biking. Always I aim for Buffalo Eddy. I don't understand what draws me, frightened as I am by this river, to this place, to the heart of chaos. Water is high again this year—double the average snowcap—but flooding is localized and the rains helpfully hold off. I'm determined to know the canyon in all its stages. I believe, since last year, that I've struck an uneasy peace with the river.

Early on, the levee is closed again. This time it doesn't stop me; I detour onto the highway and bike above the flooding. It's curious to know that beneath the murky water is the bike path, that even now blunt-headed carp are wallowing in the shallows, mouthing the asphalt surface in a long, muddy kiss.

I'm starting out with an advantage, my wind and weight good, my legs strong after the mild winter, from taking long walks with Dennis. Although walking is not comfortable—the bones in my feet are fusing and painful—nor is it easy to keep up with him—my stride as short as my legs—I believe we're both trying to find some way back to each other. Still, we inevitably end up walking apart, his step ahead of mine. He is abstracted. His gaze never settling on any one thing longer than a few moments. We talk about work. We talk about pulling my book from New York for revision. We talk about teaching. We spend great blocks of time not talking about much more than the weather. It never occurs to us to admit out loud that in the past four months we haven't said anything more or less to each other than a stranger might.

Always he is that pace or two, five feet, ten feet ahead of me, not a conscious abandonment, rather it's a reflex, an impulse like the one that keeps his gaze from mine, sets him pacing the house, a jumpiness that's driving him away faster, and farther until, finally, even a pair of roller skates I purchase from the local Goodwill can't catch me up. I get back on my bike. If I must be alone, I prefer it to be of my own choosing.

I pass beneath Swallows Nest—an enormous cliff that juts out from the rolling hillsides like the prow of a ship. The swallows have mudded the rock face—river-bottom mud—a thousand and more hollow-bodied nests piping in the wind. The river flows, hard to judge its speed. I watch a log, one of many, hurtling down the current, and it takes my breath away, hits me like a rush of adrenaline. I pedal beneath trees-of-heaven—spindly, skyward things—and past a locust grove where the grass is always greener. I spin away down the highway, through the tiny town of Asotin with its ballpark, school, gas station and rumored serial killer.

Outside of town, although the hills steepen abruptly, the river commands the view with elegant serpentines, a broad greeny swath that buckles the willow stands, scrubs a dirty foam from cottonwood roots. Magpie startle out of the cutbank, pennoned wing tips flashing, and there's the stench of something dead. Something large. While I'm surprised by the smell, I become aware of the undercurrent in the air, an infusion of decay—loess, bones, leaf marl, flesh—sweet and bitter all at once, released from the reliquary snows. A vast purging, an outpouring of old regrets.

I pedal on, paralleling the river, counter current, finding my way upstream like some unlikely fish. It's a struggle, so early in the year. I pace myself, and three quarters to the eddy I already know I will make it there and back. It will be a six-hour day, away from cares, home, husband. It is the first of many that spring. The first of a growing number of hours.

⌐ ⌐ ⌐

The river breathes. I discover this early summer. June, I think. I'm averaging 210 miles a week, mostly on this river road. The temperature is in the high eighties midcanyon and I stop often to swim, and this is new to me, the ease with which I now step into the water.

Although the river is never really warm, as my childhood lakes were, the air is so hot, so dry, my skin so beaten by the sun that I relish the cold that stings even the breath from my lungs. The waters are still unusually high, but have cleared so that I can see the five or more feet to rocky bottom. The surface is opaque with color from shoreline trees: bright aspen, the early green of dagger leaf willow, a deep spray of cottonwood. It is umber with the rocky hills, and in the bowl of the current where the choppy spume of rapids levels out it is a bright wash of sky. All color and movement.

I am happiest out here these days. I find a quiet I can't locate in my home, filled so often as it is now with friends or activity, TV or stereo, as if the two of us can't admit silence. We fall to sleep in grudges, but Dennis still ladles me into his lap so that I can drift to sleep spooned against his belly. My bike rides have become lengthy meditations. I pedal the long hours and my thoughts wheel. I contemplate the new novel I'm hard at work on—all about a woman whose marriage is unraveling in ways she cannot begin to comprehend. How the destruction of her life blindsides her.

I think about marriage, how difficult it is, the days of easy drifting, the turbulence, and at its hardest—that most ordinary eddying of passion—the time all couples come to when they bank on their accumulated years and history to tide them over, to carry them safely through to the next great flooding of heart. I love knowing a man so well that I recognize the sound of his step among many, or coming down a corridor, out of sight. I love that my heart still jumps and calms with the recognition, even after all these years, or perhaps because of it. For this deep knowing is like coming to understand some inarticulate part of myself, some capacity to respond outside of reason, the way water finds its own level.

I venture farther into the river, duck my head under through an act of will, for I have never trusted total immersion, giving it over so completely, eyes and nose and ears closed off from the known world. I open my eyes and in the murky underwater light I fight the panic—fearful I will see the things I consciously avoid thinking of when treading water, those great toothy creatures:

sturgeon, pike, or the latest dead caught in a tangle of logs, or that
thing out there I can never really know, that has chased me
up basement stairs since I was three. Immersion for me is, like
marriage, a question of faith, of trust in its possibilities, in my
husband, and more importantly in myself, believing that should I
finally see the sturgeon at my heels I will prove strong enough.

Cooled off and on my bike again, I pass the brace of rocks where
a wild mink resides. Bold little creature. He stands on hind legs, ears
pricked forward and watches as I slow. He bounds along the rocky
shore a short distance, keeping parallel, keeping me in sight. When
I stop, it is he that studies me and when satisfied dips from sight
and is gone. It is a ritual we have developed these last several weeks.

I ride beneath an osprey nest, the adult pair screaming overhead
from opposite ends of the river they circumnavigate. They are
cunning fisher birds, and it is not unusual on these rides for me to
look up and see fish torsioning, a snake coiling in their talons.

I reach one of my four favorite views, where the hills form a gap
and the river disappears in a bend. It is, I realize, the texture of
this place that engages me, the overlays of hill against hill against
distant mountains, the slender thread of river working its will.

When I reach the eddy, I clamber down to a jut of rocks freshly
revealed this past month by the river's fall, part of the basalt
archipelago that cinches the river's waist. I hop across a small side
rivulet, step over a stone bulwark to perch on top a likely
boulder—the tip of a much larger rock mass, perhaps the original
wall the river weathered through all those thousands of years ago.
I face downriver, the water rushing by on my right. It takes a
while to hear it—the steady sound of the rapids so easily
consigned to white noise—the lapse I gradually become aware of,
those few moments when the call of the gray jay bells down the
canyon and the drone of bees nestling into the blossoming lamb's
ear take on a singular clarity. I hear a moment of silence, and then
the continuance of river, and shortly thereafter yet another hush.
Pivoting on my rock as the rushing sound reappears, I become aware

of the water forging around my perch. The water is rising, subsumes the small rapids, and I become an island. It's a paltry channel that separates me from the mainland rock and over the next half minute it dribbles into nothing. And so it is the river rising and falling, rising and falling—sound and silence—like an intake and exhalation. I wonder what law of physics plays into this. I imagine the spits of land that form the eddies, the bends and bottlenecks that suspend the river's momentum until the weight and rising mass carry it in a surge to the next bend, the next eddy. Up river, downriver, it's all an interconnected system of checks and release.

Or not. It is more than that. A long, sustained, intake of breath. And release.

I am transfixed to the rock, holding on. I am giddy with discovery— as if I've stumbled onto some great secret.

But what the secret is I'm still unsure, and when I finally start the long ride home, it's not with the usual dread—the logginess that settles into my limbs as I angle back toward town, toward the slackwater, the canyon vistas closing shut behind me, the half-hearted pace I usually set—this time I travel with the current, pace myself with a brash of logs bucking their way downstream. I set my back to the wilderness and focus on the road ahead. I lose sight of the logs while climbing, gain on the downside. I swing past isolated homes, no time to wonder about their lives, what these couples speak of when they turn lights off. I pass fenced horses drowsing in the late afternoon light, cattle foraging in the sage. I speed by empty beaches, ride the gravel shoulder too close to a hundred-foot drop. I have been gone almost seven hours. I wing the last miles to tell Dennis of my discovery. I arrive downstream with the logs, and we part at the confluence. I chain my bike to the back porch and enter an empty house. I wait for Dennis. Showered and refreshed, I sit on the front stoop, a glass of ice water against my cheek. The hills take on a bruised hue. I wait, and wonder what it was I actually saw—the breath of rivers?

Or perhaps, as likely, the breath of God.

Midsummer. The day starts in an eddy. All the affairs I have put off for biking need to be attended to—summer school, preps, revision on my book, a new short story, conversation with my husband. He's surprised I'm staying home. I take it for granted that he won't argue, or try to dissuade me from leaving—all the hours I'm logging alone on the road. I've stopped wondering why. I take it as a sign of love, his willingness to give me the space and distance I seem to need these days. But like that great mass of river in the eddy, building its own slow momentum, the everyday matters threaten to spill over unless I see to them. Today, I'm housebound, but it's all right. I feel charged. My body is in fighting trim and I'm focused in a way I haven't been in years. I have energy to spare. I'll ride later, I say. Tomorrow.

Dennis is staying close. When I look up he is there, hovering, and I think of the evening before, how restless he was, turning in sleep, turning, pulling me and the blankets to him again and again. "Was it a bad night?" I ask, although I already know, having wakened with his fits and starts.

He nods. He opens his mouth to speak, closes it again. Paces off. When he comes back, he carries his distraction in his hands— fingering the counters, hands in and out of pockets, fingers raking through his hair. I wait.

"Bad dreams all night," he says.

I think of how he held me when we woke. How tenuous it felt. I want to sympathize, but I sleep well these days. Sheer exhaustion.

I am suspended in the river. My feet firm on the sandy bottom. My bike is still roadside in the gravel. I don't hear any traffic and the motorboat that caused the wake has long passed. I don't hear or see any of it. I can still feel though, how the water rocks me, and marvel at the stubbornness, the strength with which my legs and feet hold me in place. I look down the river. I feel the current so close at hand, and it becomes clear to me that I could let go.

That easy.

I could let go, give myself over to this river as I have given myself over to the events of an afternoon, the sudden unraveling of a marriage, riding the momentum of the last two years. I could let it take me where it would. There is no greater harm this water can do to me.

Earlier this morning, Dennis had suggested a walk. A short distance from home, we stood under spreading elm branches, the bright sunlight dappling the grass and concrete sidewalk. He talked— anxious patter that took a sudden serious turn, and then a dark turn and darker still, stripping away our lives together, our marriage, like flesh from bone. I stumbled where I stood. A black Lab launched himself along a picket fence, and children bolted past with backpacks slung from arms, but the day had lost all familiarity— the hills flattened beyond the trees, and the trees became a weedy tangle in air turned watery. My limbs were weightless. Though I did not believe I had closed my eyes, I felt them open. I saw my husband a stranger. I stepped back. I saw who we had been—the couple I believed in—become unrecognizable. A bird swam upward, between leaves and branches, was gone. We waited in silence, having said all we needed. Having put our twelve years of marriage to rest in the span of those bright, brief moments. I left him standing there and I made my way home alone.

I found my bike, and then I found myself here. Immersed in the Snake.

It's curious. There are no questions. No blame. I stand emptied. I hardly know myself anymore. I study my body through the wavering water, the arms that float out at my side as though they were a stranger's. I become aware of how thoroughly this river has reshaped me, how deep this new channel cuts through my heart.

I tread water. The sound of blood rushes through my ears like the hum of katydids. In a world gone out of true, I search for something certain. I know this river. There is comfort in that. I know how the hills fold against each other. I know how quickly the canyon cools once the sun fails the other side of the hills. I know the cry of a magpie slicing through the air. All of this—like a blessing. I cup my hands in the water, rinse my face. What I cannot know is what awaits me once I step out of this river. I cannot yet imagine the ride home, the angry days ahead, or the dark evenings when Dennis and I will sit at a careful distance, determining our courses, together or apart. I cannot know how we will struggle to understand the forces that undermine us—what we bring upon ourselves, what is wrought upon us. We are steeped in undercurrents, riffles and slackwater, bottomless pools and eddies. It seems I have always known this. It is the immersion, the act of will, the transcendent leap beyond the limitations of flesh and fear—call it faith—that I must learn and relearn continuously. This is a river as old as memory, older. I feel the water rise, and fall. And rise. I breathe.

Waiting for Coyote

Louise Freeman-Toole

The Nez Perce tell the story of the five swallow sisters who built
a dam that kept the salmon from migrating upriver. Coyote came
down the river and didn't like what he saw, so he turned himself
into a baby floating along in a cradleboard. When the board
washed up against the dam, he cried piteously until the sisters
found him. They fussed over the poor baby and took him home.
But the next day, while they were out digging for camas roots,
Coyote took a digging stick and started scratching at the dam, the
dirt flying out between his hind legs. He worked at it for five
days, until finally the swallows returned and caught him destroying
their handiwork. The sisters darted around Coyote, beating him
about the head. He plucked them out of the air one by one, then
calmly finished destroying the dam. From that time on, the
salmon were free to swim upriver to spawn and to provide food
for the people and bears. And Coyote made the swallow sisters
promise to build mud nests on the cliffs every spring to herald the
return of the salmon.

A few miles downriver from Asotin, Washington, Swallows Nest
looms above the Snake River like a flying buttress or the prow of
an ocean liner. It is visible for miles but only from up close can
you see the columns of basalt that form its distinctive shape. The
cliff used to be plastered with swallows' nests made of silt taken

from the wide mud flats along the river. Lower Granite Dam transformed this section of river into a reservoir that extends a mile beyond the town. The mud flats gave way to levees lined with riprap. Most of the swallows now build their nests farther upriver where the current still runs fast, lined by miles of muddy banks and undisturbed cliffs. Asotin is little more than a gas station, a school, a diner, the county historical museum, a ballpark. It's not too hard to imagine these simple buildings replaced by tepees. This flat spot at the mouth of Asotin Creek has always been a good place for people, with a year-round creek, plenty of shade, and lots of eels. *Hesutiin,* the place of the eels. Asotin is a good place to stop and refuel—a tank of gas, a candy bar—before heading upriver to my friend's ranch.

The road dead-ends at Heller Bar. To see the river before it disappears into Hells Canyon, you have to drive up and over the Salmon River Mountains of central Idaho or the Blue Mountains of Oregon. The Snake River near Weiser, in southern Idaho, looks very different from the Snake River I'm used to. The river undergoes several major changes on its way from western Wyoming. It flows over eleven dams before it reaches my friend's ranch and eight more before it reaches the ocean. In southern Idaho, the Snake sometimes disappears entirely. One hundred percent of the river is allocated to meet the demands for irrigation and city water to the growing towns around Boise and Twin Falls. In low flow years, the river is sucked dry. Miles downriver, it is reconstituted, like cheap orange juice, from treated wastewater, tanks at the local trout farms. The extra nutrients encourage the growth of algae, which forms a green scum on the surface of the slow-moving water behind Brownlee Dam. Yet the old-timers assure me that the river is cleaner than it was when untreated sewage was released directly into the river. Back in the old days, one said, it was "a running sewer full of moss and bugs and trash fish."

The Snake River doesn't really recover until it passes through Hells Canyon. Gathering speed as it falls in elevation, it aerates and cleanses itself as it tumbles over the rocks. Infusions of clean water enter from the Salmon River on the Idaho side, and the

Imnaha and Grande Ronde on the Oregon side. Between Hells
Canyon and Lower Granite, the first dam below Lewiston, Idaho,
there is a 110-mile gap. The stretch that includes my friend's ranch
is the longest remaining free-flowing section of the Snake. It's the
gap—that precious 110-mile gap—that I care so much about.

⌐ ⌐ ⌐

The canyon is empty today. There are no boats on the river, no
cars on the road. I love this time of year when even the swallows
have gone. The sky is clouded over and water is a still, silvery
green. Spots of color are vivid against the muted background:
yellow willows along the shore, brilliant green moss on the rocks,
red sumac in the side canyons. A lone steelhead fisherman wades
out into the water, arms raised as if going to meet a dancing
partner.

I know I never will share a fisherman's love of water. I'll never be a
river-runner, like those who float down the Salmon and on
into the Snake, taking their rubber rafts, dories, and kayaks out at
Heller Bar, where the road ends (or begins, depending which
direction you're headed). Never mind that I took swimming
lessons every year of my childhood, and that I learned to water-
ski, handle a dinghy, and drive a ski boat. It makes little difference
that I had surfer boyfriends with chapped lips and callused knees,
a brother who jogged down the beach every morning with a squad
of Junior Lifeguards, a father who learned to mend sails in the
Navy, and Yankee trader forefathers who sailed all the way to the
Far East. No matter that we explored tidepools on the Palos
Verdes peninsula and camped on the beach in Baja; that we made
sojourns to the freshwater lakes of Lake Shasta and Clear Lake;
the man-made reservoirs of Lake Elsinore, Pyramid Lake,
Lake Piru, Castaic Lake, Lake Cachuma, Nacimiento Reservoir, Lake
Isabella, Pine Flat Reservoir; the saline waters of Mono Lake,
Salton Sea, Great Salt Lake; the mountain waters of the Kings,
Kern, American, Truckee, Tuolomne rivers; and the desert
shores of the Colorado. Despite the fact that I spent most of my
childhood near, on, or in water, I remain, stubbornly, a land person.

Although I have not been drawn to water, neither have I been afraid of it. My father made sure of that. When we first got our little dinghy, he took the five oldest kids out in the boat, leaving my mom standing on the shore, my baby sister in her arms, my little brother by her side. We rowed out to the middle of the lake. At my father's signal, we gripped the sides of the boat and started rocking back and forth, delirious with anticipation. Finally, with a wild grin, he started counting. "One." He leaned to the right. Screams of delight. "Two." He threw his weight to the left. And then "Three—" We were cut off in midscream as the lake heaved up with a cold smack and we found ourselves upside-down in the dark green water. Our life jackets popped us to the surface like orange balloons. We dog-paddled around the overturned dinghy while onshore several men raced for their boats until my mother waved them away, calling out, "They're fine, they're fine." The men stood on the sand, watching, and a small crowd gathered as we worked together to right the boat. We hauled each other in and rowed back to camp. The men laughed, "You had us scared for a minute there," and the women shook their heads and smiled at my mom as if she were the brave one.

All the more surprising, then, that I am often afraid of crossing the Snake. Even after years of rowing across to the ranch on the Idaho side of the river, the prospect of making that crossing lends a low level of anxiety to what would otherwise be a very peaceful drive. Even as I follow the curves of this familiar road, I'm thinking already about getting from point A to point B before the current carries me to point Z somewhere down around Lewiston. When I first launch one of the rowboats that belong to the ranch, my attention is taken up with bailing, maneuvering out into the river and getting oriented, setting a rhythm. But then, about midway, I'm sometimes overtaken by a fear so strong it's almost paralyzing. My mouth goes dry. My arms are weak. The oars go every which way. Rushing water sounds suddenly behind my back, as if a whirlpool has just formed ahead of the boat. I glance nervously over my shoulder, and it's just the creek, tumbling down the rocky bank, telling me to steer slightly north so I will land on the beach.

I've never attempted to row myself across the Snake at spring flood, but have sat very still in the back of the boat while a friend rowed and logs and chunks of ice barreled past, a kaleidoscope of whirlpools forming and unforming around us. Equally as dangerous as the whirlpools are the boils that can well up suddenly from beneath, spitting out huge chunks of debris that can knock an oar out of your hand, batter your boat, spin you around in the rushing water, disoriented. But the river is nothing now compared to what it used to be in the spring. Now much of the water is held back behind the three upriver dams to fill the reservoirs for the summer months. Before the dams, the spring snow melt charged down the canyon at between 50,000 and 70,000 cubic feet per second, almost five times as much as today's flow.

The thought of anyone attempting to cross the river in that kind of flood is almost inconceivable. And yet, thirty-five miles upriver is the point, marked now by a small sign, where Chief Joseph's band of Nez Perce was forced to cross the Snake at spring flood. At that time of year, the runoff from the high country of the Wallowas and the Seven Devils is cold enough to stop a person's heart. Homesteaders who had steadily encroached upon the Nez Perce homeland in the stunningly beautiful Wallowa Valley wanted the Indians out. Joseph's band was given just a few weeks to round up their cattle from what is now southeastern Oregon, pack their possessions, get across the Snake River, and make their way to the reservation at Lapwai, Idaho. Nez Perce families loaded their possessions into bullboats made of hide. Over six thousand head of cattle and horses were herded into the swift water. Hundreds of men, women, old people and children crossed the river on horseback or in the round boats. Some of the stock drowned, but, incredibly, no human lives were lost.

My rancher friend, now retired, often has told me about the Nez Perce who used to come to camp alongside the creek when he was a boy.

"Why did they stop coming?"

"No fish," he said. "Got Brownlee Dam built up there and it stopped the chinook runs long before these other dams were thought about."

Brownlee went into operation in 1959. Within the next couple of years, the number of salmon caught in a night of dipnetting went from fifteen or twenty to maybe one, sometimes none.

Not far from where I eventually land the boat, there are three waist-high rock walls that have stood for centuries. They look like terraced garden walls angling toward the river. The ancestors of the Nez Perce used to anchor their boats over the walls and net the fish as they came upriver. Over the years, as silt from the creek built up the bank, the river gradually moved west, leaving the rock structures high and dry. The Indians would then build a new wall, parallel to the old one. Now the river covers the lowest, newest wall only in the spring when the water is very high. If the salmon still ran in great numbers and the Nez Perce still came to their traditional fishing site near the mouth of the creek, it might be about time to build a new fish wall.

In the spring of 1992, a trial "drawdown" was conducted at Lower Granite and Little Goose dams to see if it was feasible to lower reservoir levels each spring to help young salmon reach the sea more quickly. The release of more water from behind the dams would reduce the amount of time the smolts spent in the reservoirs, where they were vulnerable to the higher water temperatures and warm-water predators such as squawfish. For the first time in almost twenty years, the river ran swiftly in a narrow channel. Long-buried structures and landforms began to reappear. Rotting pilings. A rock formation called Cabbage Head. Nez Perce landmarks: a rock called Coldweather Girl where Winter's daughter stood in the water; a waterfall formed when Coyote extended his penis across the river to impress some girls. Mud flats. Cars. Dead fish. Gravel bars. Tires. Fishing gear. Forgotten swimming holes. An island once connected to downtown Lewiston by a footbridge, where families would sit on bleachers to watch baseball games. An office safe. Handguns. Human bones. Another island, one that housed a tent city of hoboes in the 1930s. A calm back eddy where children used to ice-skate in winter. Docks cracking from their own weight. Swallows dipping up mud to plaster nests on the basalt cliffs. A river playing music again.

Unfortunately, without enough water to support new structures such as docks, millions of dollars of damage was done. Those dependent on the reservoir system—farmers who relied on barges to get their grain to market, the pulp mill, the boating industry— called the drawdown a "colossal failure." Even the proponents of the plan were daunted by the cost of repairs. What was supposed to have been the beginning of a series of drawdowns became a one-time experiment.

The fish biologist at the Idaho Department of Fish and Game office in Lewiston briefed me on the salmon recovery efforts that had recently allowed a limited season on chinook salmon for the first time in twenty years. He was just another bureaucrat spouting statistics until I asked him what it had been like to participate in that rare season on the Clearwater River. His eyes lit up as he struggled to describe the feel of that salmon on the end of his line, "Like nothing I've ever experienced before." I asked, "Do you think there's any hope for the salmon?" He said, seriously but with that light still in his eyes, "Yes, I do. I have to believe that. Otherwise I wouldn't be able to come to work every day."

There are three dams on the Middle Snake: Brownlee, Oxbow, and Hells Canyon. Commuter flights between Lewiston and Boise routinely fly over Hells Canyon and the dams are easy to spot: Brownlee, one of the largest rock-fill dams in the world, looks huge even from 23,000 feet; just a short distance downriver is Oxbow Dam, placed at an omega-shaped bend in the river; Hells Canyon, wedged between cliffs about 600 feet apart, appears as a tiny cinch pulling the canyon tight. In the reservoirs behind each dam, the Snake lies bloated and sluggish, covering the canyon floor. Below Hells Canyon Dam, the river shrinks to a bright ribbon winding back and forth across the bottom of the canyon, with beaches, islands, and gravel bars. I try to imagine the river as it looked before the dams, when there were four times as many beaches in Hells Canyon. A longtime resident of Asotin told me, "What everyone used to remark on about the Snake was all the white sand beaches." Now the silt gets trapped behind the dams, and the daily, even hourly, fluctuation of the water level eats away at the riverbank.

Like the eight dams on the Lower Snake and the Columbia, these three on the Middle Snake have had a catastrophic effect on the salmon runs. Salmon are the megafauna of the Northwest, and they appear as iconic figures everywhere from art galleries to tackle shops. Colorful sockeyes and muscular chinook appear—tails flipped—on hats, T-shirts, billboards, and the covers of sportfishing magazines. You can find salmon-shaped pencil holders, flower vases, hat racks, wall sconces, serving platters. Salmon restoration efforts have cost hundreds of millions of dollars and have caused more debate than any other issue in the Northwest. But with all the focus on salmon, the decline of other species often has been overlooked.

Eels, too, once swarmed up the river every spring, and sturgeon cruised hundreds of miles out into the ocean and back again. Sturgeon are large, primitive-looking beasts that have survived, virtually unchanged, for over 200 million years. Over a lifetime that could span a hundred years, a sturgeon might travel dozens of times up and down the Columbia River system and out into the ocean, going as far north as the coast of Alaska. At the turn of the century it was not uncommon for a commercial fisherman to haul in his setline and find a twelve-foot-long sturgeon weighing over seven hundred pounds. Most of the sturgeon caught now are under five feet in length. Fish experts speculate that without the spawned-out salmon, there aren't enough nutrients in the river for the sturgeon to grow to record size. Or perhaps the sturgeon eventually get too big to negotiate the fish ladders on the lower Snake and Columbia River dams. Nowadays, it is illegal to remove sturgeon from the water; fishermen will hold one alongside the boat, admiring its retractable shovel snout and the razor sharp ridges on its back, until it catches its breath. They let it go, hoping that someday their children, or even their great-grandchildren, will catch that same fish, grown to the size of a canoe.

Everywhere you go along the Snake River, there are old pictures of sturgeon: hanging out the back of a wagon, tail almost touching the ground; a girl sitting on a saddle cinched around a sturgeon as big as a pony; a sturgeon hanging from a beam, dwarfing the man beside it. And there are stories, too. The fish a homesteader caught that was so heavy that he hitched up his horse and boy to haul the thing out of the water and almost lost both stock and child when the monster made a run for the deep. Nez Perce accounts tell of "sociable" sturgeons that would swim close to children in the water, or, like a friendly dolphin, offer a fin to take a drowning person to the surface. Sturgeon even took on the dimensions of Paul Bunyan's blue ox, Babe. In this tale—which many old-timers swore happened to someone they knew—a miner harnessed a sturgeon to two railroad ties, stood on the ties, the rope wrapped around one fist like a rodeo wrap, and rode that thing "from Brownlee to Copperfield."

I've never seen a sturgeon, but I heard one surface behind me when I was rowing across the river. I heard it blow and roll like a sea beast. The other woman in the boat looked over my shoulder and yelled, "What the hell is that?" like she'd caught a glimpse of old Nessie herself. Canyon residents speak of being awakened by the slap of a sturgeon surfacing, so loud it echoes against the cliffs.

My father and brothers used to go deep sea fishing from a barge out in Santa Monica Bay. They would bring home a barracuda with a jutting jawful of teeth, a halibut with both eyes on one side of its head, or a red snapper with a bladder of air protruding from its mouth. Occasionally, a fish would have a circular scar on its side: the mark of a moray eel. The single most disturbing picture in our *Encyclopedia Americana*—even worse than photos of rare skin diseases—was a photo of a moray eel's mouth lined with a circlet of jagged teeth. A moray eel was a nightmare creature, a leach with the teeth of a piranha.

Eels once made their way up fast-moving creeks like Asotin Creek by clinging first to one boulder and then another. Nez Perce boys harvested the eels by pulling them off the rocks, being careful not to grab them too far back along the neck. An eel with too much wiggle room could whip around and attach itself to a boy's arm, leaving that ugly circular scar. The Nez Perce used to dry the eels in small smokehouses built in the thorn bushes along the creek. Sometimes they roasted them like hot dogs over a fire. They'd curl an eel around a green stick and hold it over the fire until the dripping grease made the flames flare up, hissing.

Suckerfish were another favorite, despite their numerous bones. The Nez Perce cooked them in a pit lined with rocks and covered with sand. In the old days, after a long winter of dried fish, roots and berries, and surviving on moss soup when food grew short, the Nez Perce must have welcomed the arrival of the suckers—the first fish to come up the river in early spring. I would have liked to have been there on the beach when a suckerfish was dug from the hot sand, to see the skull fall apart into separate pieces, and to hear the stories about how the tiny, intricately shaped bones came to be called "Grizzly's earring," "Raven's socks," and "Cricket packing her child."

It didn't matter that eels were a staple of the Nez Perce's traditional diet; to the Army Corps of Engineers, they were merely pests. The Corps installed iron bars to keep morays out of the fish ladders around the dams. Now the eels have stopped coming.

⌒ ⌒ ⌒

The fish were not the only things affected by the dams. The character of the river has been changed in many ways, large and small. Longtime residents of the canyon sometimes talk about the old days when the river used to freeze in winter. Ever since the three upriver dams were built, the Snake no longer freezes. The water released from Hells Canyon dam stays at a relatively constant temperature. But even now, "It doesn't get cold like that anymore," the old-timers say, remembering the winter of 1948, when the paddle wheel *Florence* got stuck in the ice and hay had to be flown in and airdropped to feed the stock. Unable to get their supplies by boat, ranch families would drive their horses across, pulling sleds loaded with groceries and other necessities. The first time I heard one of these stories, I imagined a couple taking a cozy ride across smooth ice, tucked beneath a buffalo robe, bells ringing on the horses' harnesses. But it wasn't like that at all. The ice would break up and then refreeze, forming treacherous pressure ridges. The horses would often panic on the slippery surface and plunge through the ice, cutting the flesh on their legs to ribbons.

There is a sadness in the storytellers' voices, not because they miss those days of hardship and cold, but because the world is changing in unfathomable ways. The weather is doing strange things. Farmers, who used to be heroes for feeding the world, are now being criticized for overproduction and blamed for causing erosion and water pollution. The need to control predators was once unquestioned, but now the national forests are being handed back to the wolves and the bears. The very idea of progress is being turned on its head. What many had thought was unthinkable—breaching the dams—is being debated at town meetings and in letters to the editor.

Many area residents remember how the "feds" had come and talked them into building the dams in the first place, back in the sixties. Yes, orchards would be bulldozed, houses moved, Nez Perce burial sites flooded, but it would all be worth it. The dams would bring progress and prosperity to the region. Jobs would be generated just as surely as hydroelectricity from the turbines. Dam builders even then knew that salmon would be adversely affected, but they downplayed that issue and focused on the increased opportunities for sportfishing in the reservoirs: smallmouth bass! crappie! (both non-native, warm-water species).

Now the federal government has made an about-face, telling locals that progress is "back thataway"—back to the days of the free-flowing river. To protect endangered runs of salmon and to honor Indian fishing rights guaranteed by treaty, the dams might have to go. At a local town meeting about salmon restoration, a Palouse farmer stood up and shouted, "They talk about a free-flowing river! Doesn't anyone remember what the river was like before the dams? It was dangerous, there was no access, bust the bottom of your boat on it!" His words echoed those of another man who'd just declared that if it weren't for the farmers, the land would be "just like it was when the Indians were here. They wouldn't have done a damn thing with it."

I stopped following the debate, lost in the thought of the Snake River and the Palouse hills before a "damn thing" had been done to them.

Mary Jim, one of the last members of the Palouse tribe to live along the Lower Snake, remembered what it was like before the dams. The river once "played music to my people," she said in a newspaper interview many years ago, "but now the river is silent."

What would it be like to have that sound silenced? I try to imagine my childhood nights without the fall of waves on the beach. I can't imagine it. The sound swung me in my sleep like a hammock. It was there after the TV was turned off and my mother stopped clattering the dinner dishes. It rose to fill the silence left after my father had ended his day with *Night on Bald Mountain* or *The 1812 Overture,* turned up so loud the floor shook. I heard it most clearly in the gray hour just before sunrise, but it was there in the background throughout the day, ever-present as the ocean breeze that blew the curtain in our bathroom window. And I knew that the sound of waves had been there through my mother's childhood, my father's childhood, my grandmother's childhood. And it had been there throughout my great-grandfather's decade as an invalid with heart disease, reclining on a wicker chaise longue on the porch, years passing with little change except the face of the nurse who bent over him to tuck a blanket around his legs.

☞ ☞ ☞

In 1958, the Army Corps of Engineers recommended that a dam be built at Asotin. The dam wasn't needed for power generation, but it would make it possible for barges to reach a major limestone deposit on the Idaho side. With all the dams being built on the Columbia River system, the Corps figured with a kind of circular logic, they were going to need that limestone to make cement. Congress gave the go-ahead for the Asotin dam in 1962. The twenty-six-mile reservoir would back up slackwater all the way from Asotin to the confluence of the Snake and Salmon rivers. The river level would rise fifty feet, covering every building on my friend's ranch, as well as the garden, the winter pastures, the barns and corrals. A team of archaeologists set up camp at the ranch while they worked to recover artifacts from the area that would be inundated.

> During the survey we recorded a limited number of historic sites. Many more exist in and adjacent to the Asotin Reservoir area. These include mines, quarries, lime kilns, school houses, ranches, sawmills, and pioneer graves. We believe that some provision should be made for locating, describing, and photographing these sites of historic interest before they are destroyed.
>
> —Archeological Survey and Test,
> Asotin Dam Reservoir Area, Southeastern Washington, 1964

In addition to the dam planned at Asotin, dams were "contemplated" at four more sites upriver from my friend's ranch: Nez Perce, China Gardens, High Mountain Sheep, and Lower Canyon. Sportfishermen and environmentalists—two groups who were seldom in agreement—came together in the middle sixties to oppose the dams and to build support for the creation of the Hells Canyon National Recreation Area. The recreation area came into being in 1975—the same year that slackwater reached Lewiston as the reservoir filled behind just-completed Lower Granite Dam.

Although Asotin was beyond the borders of the recreation area, Congress decided to reverse its earlier decision and de-authorize the dam project. Thirteen years after getting the go-ahead, the Army Corps of Engineers were forced to abandon their plans for a dam at Asotin.

Private power companies were quick to realize that the clause prohibiting dam construction at Asotin applied only to federally funded projects. Plans for a privately built dam were put back on the drawing board, and the issue continued to be debated through the rest of the seventies and most of the eighties. Finally, in 1988, the court ruled that no how, no way, was any dam—federal or private—going to be built at Asotin. After thirty years, the threat to my friend's ranch is gone.

☙ ☙ ☙

After spending the day hiking up side canyons to take photos, it's time for me to cross the river again. I walk through the orchard to say good-bye to my friend. The last of the light leaves early from the canyon at this time of year. The sky is a seamless gray—a gray stolen from the river that's now in shadow. A few out-of-reach pears are faintly visible, pale bulbs that might blink on like streetlights any minute now. The cold is moving down from the mountain. From my friend's house comes a warm yellow light and the sound of an old piano, brittle as dry leaves underfoot. I step to the porch and stop at the sight of the old man's hunched back, swaying as his hands romp up and down the keyboard. Long underwear shows through a worn place on the back of his shirt. There's a fire in the woodstove. I stand watching him, reluctant to interrupt. But I need to get across the river before it's completely dark. I knock on the window and wave.

He hollers hello and motions me in. I open the door and step into a room warm and bright and smelling of winter pears. I thank whoever there is to thank that this place, this person, this moment was not located, described, photographed, then destroyed.

The rancher walks me down to the river. I'd read improbable accounts of sturgeon rising out of the water, ghostly and white, and I ask if he'd ever seen such a thing. "Yup, there was one used to come up regular when we were crossing. Just curious, I guess. Always along about dusk, 'bout this time of day here. They just rise up about three, four feet out of the water, maybe ten feet away from your boat and just eyeball you for a minute, then slip back down without a splash or anything. Scared hell out of some people—thought the devil was after 'em." He laughs, then is silent for a minute. "It's a sight that'll stir the soul."

⌒ ⌒ ⌒

Coyote has disappeared. No one knows where he is anymore. The Nez Perce believe he will come again. His return will signal a change for the world. Coyote will destroy the dams and the forests will stand again. It will be a time of reconciliation and healing. Everyone on earth—all the generations that have gone before and all that will come after—will live together as one people.

They are still waiting for Coyote.

In the Presence of the Clearwater

Gary Gildner

I

Walking this Idaho land I live on, I hear wind brushing through big conifers, a pine cone falling branch by branch—*pwak! pwak!*—a tree creaking over an inch, a tumbling rock knocking against other rocks, the sudden flutter of a chukar's wings, and the South Fork of the Clearwater rushing down cold from Elk City—all great and modest actions, adventures inevitable and fine. Don't stop, my heartbeat says, don't stop.

Far off, I hear Sparky whinny. I step on a fir twig, crack it, am given one clear individual note—punctuation in a jumpy sentence—and think of Thelonious Monk stripping melody down to its essentials. Or it's the finger-snapping sound I remember my leg making, breaking, as I slid into third base all those years ago. A crow's harsh caw goes up. Then nothing for a while. Then a wild turkey's outraged fussy complaint. Then only my heartbeat, tha-thumpa, tha-thumpa, that little rubber drum a kid is happy to beat, keeping time, on his determined way somewhere.

Sparky whinnies again. He belongs to Grover, my neighbor, who takes him elk hunting. Grover walks, Sparky carries the pack. They are a pair of toothy old sunburned grunts, Grover will say, pressing his grizzled cheek into Sparky's: "Look at us and tell the difference."

I make my way down from the high timber toward Grover's place, but halfway there I veer off. A large punky stump I know in a sunny clearing—around which blackberry bushes push up from the rocky soil in abundant sprawl for the bears to come and get fat on—is where I want to sit for a spell, and whittle, and watch the river.

I can watch it for a long time, even at a distance, and get lost and located simultaneously, and on this day I am soon carried over airy bright rips of spray to lathered horses I have known, how like fresh-crushed oats they always smelled, how the hard block of salt I chipped a sliver off—from the cup their tongues licked out— tasted hot. Then I am wearing a cast on my leg, using a straightened wire hanger to ease down the length of it to get at the itch. Then I hear, standing behind a furnace, the hiss of a water pipe, and feel Delphine Bononi's woolly rabbit-fur sweater pressing my heartbeat. I am in the seventh grade. No perfect tumble into sleep after fierce play, no race to raise my arm and shout from the highest, most willowy limb, no dive daring my hilarious lungs to hold out, hold out against the water's weight— not one of the world's roaring gifts that I knew compared to this, my first real kiss.

It changed the meaning of my mouth, the way I took small or great breaths forever, and if only for an instant it flares in the rippling mountain heat surrounding me, alive as anything given up wholly to a pure shimmer already slipping away, intact as nothing I can hold, a current leaving—and leaving behind, in the bright bone oven of my aging skull—one cool, finny, adolescent shiver.

Moments later I have to laugh, remembering the fiery sulfurous stink and sad, shriveled-up look of my leg after the cast came off. Then in the sunny clearing where I sit, a single honeybee declares itself to the slim Canadian thistles, to that purple blossom Sparky loves to eat, working his lips like the toothless old. I watch the bee swaying, taking its drink, while overhead a red-tailed hawk soars slowly, slowly under our brazen sun, over the South Fork's careless purpose.

For all this, I thank and praise the river, if those are the right words, and despite my urge to descend farther, to get closer to it, I can manage only to slip off the stump and ease myself into a prone posture of utter luxury, of near floating, using the soft composting fir for a pillow. I can hear the river, and that's rich enough right now. I am a citizen of that country where flow and swirl and sift produce, over and over, the perfect anthem and its response. Please do not salute yesterday or tomorrow too much, it says.

The truth is, I harbor sweet envy toward the river. Who can compose and sing like that? And carry on? And flout, caress, turning you to the moment? The subtleties in the song seem so easy. It copies no one, does not have the clicky tic for instant information, asks for no stars pinned to its bib, needs no diploma, no curriculum vitae, no fashionable shoe. Standing at our bedroom window, Lizzie and I can see a passage of it, a section of curled brilliance that on moony nights sounds like a woman removing and collecting in her palm, dreamily, a long string of favored pearls.

"Listen," one of us always says.

II

The first summer we lived on our mountain, Lizzie and I put in our first garden, on a knoll close to the house. I turned over the soil with a spade—an act, it was shocking to realize, I hadn't performed since I was a boy in Michigan. I shoveled up all the good aged-black horse manure from behind the barn and we spread it on the knoll. We also spread some steer manure from our neighbor Fred's pasture down the mountain. I bought a tiller and went over the ground again, making it look like dark brown sugar. Then using old unpainted barn siding, we built three raised beds. We left space below the lowest bed for a sandbox. When we got thirsty, we drank from the spigot at our well—water that tastes like water, straightforward as spring. We planted carrots, spinach, beets, and peas, plus a dozen Early Girl tomato plants from Rickman's Nursery in town.

"Fence up yet?" Alice Rickman asked.

We didn't have a fence up. We had two lengths of two-by-fours nailed together in a cross, the long end stuck in the ground, the cross-piece fitted out with one of my sweat-ripe shirts and a pair of gloves, and an old Tigers baseball cap fixed where a head ought to be.

"That might keep the rascals off," Alice said. "For a time anyway."

So around the knoll Lizzie and I put up a non-climb field fence, hung on ten-foot larch poles. To anchor the poles, I dug two-foot holes—eleven of them. Probably I should have dug at least three more, but those eleven took me almost half the summer. Right under the topsoil, dammit, ran a vein of granite exactly where I wanted to run my fence.

I worked on the holes every day after lunch—while the sun shone and the garden grew. My main tool became a homemade pile driver, a length of iron pipe filled with concrete. Straddling the target on my knees, I thrust the pipe down like a spear, chipping away at my mountain. Some days I was mad Ahab—or an Olympic athlete in a new, slow, sweaty event over which the TV sponsors, seeing their audience yawn, lost hair.

The holes dug, Lizzie helped me fill them with soupy cement, then helped stick in the larch poles. Two days later, everything firm, we began hanging the fence. Margaret, strapped in her stroller and wrapped to her eyes like a Slovak baby (we'd conceived her in the Tatra Mountains, the year the Czechs and Slovaks split up), watched us or snoozed.

The six-foot fencing came in fifty-foot rolls. We measured our knoll to take exactly three of them. After nailing one end of the first roll on a pole, I scooched it to the next pole, where Lizzie hooked into the wire with two claw hammers about a foot apart and, using the pole as a fulcrum, pulled hard, holding the tension, while I nailed in fence staples between her hammers. Then she moved them up the pole another foot for me to staple there.

"A couple can get to know each other on a job like this," she said.

"Having fun?"

"You ever hang fence with a woman before?"

"Not that I recall."

"It's kind of sexy. All this holding tight and so forth."

"I'm glad your mother can't hear her former cheerleader-sorority girl-Junior League daughter talk like this."

"Anyway, if you have, keep it to yourself."

We took three afternoons—one per side—to hang the fence around the triangular-shaped garden. We could have done it in half the time, but the job and our pauses were too rich to rush. In one pause we gathered up Margaret, snacks, and our bathing suits and went down to the river, to wade in off a small beach, get closer to the subtleties—that humming, a rainbow nosing by, pebbles plump and bright as mushrooms on the bottom. The baby, reaching, wanted more. I took her hands, held her up and slowly let her down, up and down, her tiny feet and mine together in a row. She squealed to see hers big, then small, then smaller. On the beach, Lizzie crawled in circles, clawing up a castle. "Maybe I am dreaming after all," she said.

In another pause, a corollary to the first, Lizzie would sit against a larch pole and nurse Margaret, positioning herself to keep her

breast, though not Margaret's eyes, in the sun. I would dump a
cup of drinking water over my head and lie back among the
tomato plants, inhaling the mixed scent of milk, pine boughs, and
those spicy green leaves brushing my ears. "I like this," she said. I
listened to the sucks of outright pleasure, the easing off from one
nipple, the arrival at the other. "I wonder if Gerard Manley
Hopkins ever considered that a good example of sprung rhythm,"
I said once, and she said, "Like to try it?"

The West, contrary to cowboy lore, is not all reticence.

"Hey!"

I glanced up.

"Easy, buster."

III

The main purpose of the fence was to keep deer off our vegetables,
but when spring came again and in the raised beds tiny spikes of
green appeared, and the morning glories wound in the wire pulsed
up and started to push out those pastel cups, and the sun sliding
over Blacktail Ridge picked out the single drop of water clinging
to the well spigot and created a large bristling effect not unlike
heat lightning, I thought I might just open the gate and whistle
the rascals in, to compare horns, to stamp my front hooves as they
do—breathing the nutty odor of musk in the making that would
drive us all—and surely it would—a little bit crazy about ourselves.

Those seeds produced. The carrots and beets were small but tall on
flavor. The peas and spinach did even better. The Early Girls did
the best. You can forget what real taste is after you've been eating
those blatant frauds hauled over the highway in chilled darkness.

As for the sandbox, I took two ten-foot larch poles that I didn't
dig holes for—the smoothest two—sawed them in half, and laid

down a square. Then we brought up sand from our favorite
neighborhood beaches. It is all fine stuff, full of the sun's brassy
swirl and the earth's rhythmic sift, like a lot of things around here.
Margaret, beginning her toddle, falls joyously in the middle, grips
little fistfuls of it, and says with her huzzahs: Yes, we may
continue.

A very good word, *continue,* and from such a nice family.
Continual, continuance, geese flying over again, right over our
flapping arms, crossing the river and its glister and all these
flickering grains. What could be more graciously willful? Lizzie
and I have no trouble getting into this pleasure from time to
time—there's plenty of room—and when we come out, as if from
a rapids, we're ravenous.

River People

Guy Hand

FEBRUARY 26, 1997: I hardly recognize the thin, sere look of this place. The California spring I left behind was awash in poppies, paintbrush, and shooting stars; the grass green; the air summer sweet. Here the air smells of frost, the ground is brittle, the riverbank faintly scratched with colors I have to push my face against to see. Pale yellows, like this winter sun, and faint rusts (colored more by my imagination than any sort of native pigment) cling to the bare branches of plants whose names I can't recall— all thrown together with the unsettling notion that I'm a native here and a newcomer all at once.

Shadows are illusory: the banks of the Boise River are caught in the diffuse light that comes before snow. Cottonwood trunks are modeled not by the play of sun against shade, but by the dark stain of an earlier rain, their limbs silhouetted only by the dusky leaves that pool on the ground beneath them. I walk tentatively— no longer accustomed to this light, this cold, this clutter of downed leaves—like a tourist wandering the beach in dress shoes. With each step, ice hidden beneath the duff cracks like bone. I consider turning back, but then catch a flash of water through the trees.

I break through to a river the color of scrap tin, a blank, heatless gray that mimics the sky. No rapids or even ripples complicate its surface as it moves swiftly through the wood and pastureland east of town. It flows silently, surreptitiously, as if not to draw attention to itself.

It draws me.

Yet the rush of water swings and swerves in all the wrong places; old landmarks—boulders, gravel bars, sandy washes—have vanished; the island I remember floating just off shore is gone. I try to recall when I was last here, but can't. (My trips to Boise have been a jumble over the past few years, occasioned less often by birthdays and summer vacations than late night phone calls and hastily packed bags.)

I walk downstream and soon the hiss of water moving into a stand of young willows breaks the silence. Their trunks tremble. The current has worked deep into these trees and only then does the high water register and I begin to understand that the river of my memory is underwater, drowned. I turn toward the place it should be, push my hands deep into my pockets, and stare at this blunt, impenetrable surface. I had hoped, in running to the Boise River, to find something of the everlasting (or at least familiar) in a town flooded with change. I stare for a long time. I stare because it's all I can think to do. It's cold and nearly dark and just three days ago my mother died.

☞ ☞ ☞

When the news came and I rushed home, I found her life suspended in air, as if between heartbeats. Everything was there: the pink robe, her scent still fresh in its fabric; a magazine opened to a story half-read; just-ripe bananas clustered in a bowl; a container of milk, fresh and waiting. Everything but her. I walked from room to room, disbelieving. Only within the pages of her calendar, where she had made meticulous daily notes, was the proof of her absence made manifest. Her inky jottings had been as regular as footprints in snow, but on the evening of the ambulance, they disappeared, leaving only the white emptiness of endless blank days.

I remembered holding her hand on the afternoon of my father's funeral; I remembered how strange, how extraordinary that small hand felt as it rested within my own, as delicate, as charged with life as a marsh wren or the spring's first lily. My mother and I seldom held hands, and on that day I was as comforted by the tenacity of her pulse as I am now unprepared for its stopping. My mother's heart attack came only a couple of years after my father's hard death, and as the older of two children, with none of my own, I felt as if I'd stumbled to the far edge of family history. I wasn't ready to inherit the house I'd grown up in, the silence it now contained, or the Idaho winter that enveloped it. I had been, in that space between heartbeats, orphaned.

At her funeral reception, familiar faces and old stories chased the silence away for a few sweet moments. My brother and his family, who had also moved from Idaho, were there, as well as aunts, uncles, cousins, and friends who'd never left. They filled the house with food and flowers and the frequently forgotten awareness that I belong to a clan. But when I found one of them in the garage, reading the odometer of my mother's car, asking if we planned to sell it, I knew then that I was a very long way from ready to erase the imprint of my parents' lives. I gave him a look that showed it, and as soon as everyone had gone, I headed for the river.

⌐ ⌐ ⌐

That this is where I come to mourn surprises me. My relationship to the Boise River, when I lived here twenty years ago, was mostly indirect and passive. I took the river for granted, wandered its banks half-conscious of its meanders, saw it as too tame, too urban, too much the sugar beet-and-potato river it becomes in the farmland west of town. For me, the Boise had little of the allure, and less of the length and complexity of the Snake or the Payette (rivers that border its watershed like liquid parentheses). The silvery flash of wildness I saw in sections of those rivers was quickly dimmed in the Boise by the three dams that block its flow shortly after it tumbles from the ice and rock of the Sawtooth Mountains.

Yet, I do remember standing here at Barber Park on the summer day my father brought his freshly transplanted Twin Falls family to the river for the first time. We came not with fly rods, but old inner tubes, and the Boise flowed by as deep and darkly unknowable as my family's future. My brother and I plunged in, teeth clenched against the cold, eyes wide and full of cottonwood leaves and sunlight. We watched as our burly, former-cowboy and soon-to-be-head-of-the-Idaho-state-police dad dropped like an upturned spider into his tube—all chalky-white arms and legs and bright, smiling face. We floated down the river wrapped in a familial bond that would never again be as closely drawn. As we paddled ashore at Ann Morrison Park, Mom met us with a flurry of clean towels, a picnic basket, and a smile made radiant by its rarity. The taste of fried chicken and macaroni salad mingled with the scent of river and freshly cut grass. It was a day, seen through this lens of loss, as sun struck and wondrous as love can allow.

That day sends a shiver from the past straight up my spine. The blue-gray mountains of the Boise Front melt into cloud. The light fades. The temperature drops. Snow begins to fall. Still, I feel warmth away from a house where everywhere I look I see only endings.

FEBRUARY 27: I got myself lost on a trip to the grocery store this morning; the kind of lost a map can't fix. Four decades ago, our house was an outpost on the southwestern frontier of town: I could step from the back porch into a sea of sage that covered the Snake River Plain in gray-green and dust to the far, rumpled horizon of the Owyhee Mountains. Now it's the city that rolls to those mountains, immersing the house in a sea of malls, multiplexes, one-hour photo labs, and newborn housing developments. At the spot where two dirt roads once intersected (a fine place, at the time, to pick blackberries) a cloverleaf interchange has risen like some concrete leviathan, devouring older homes in the neighborhood as well as the last of the open land. Boise, someone at the funeral mentioned, is the fourth fastest growing city in the country and it looks it.

Only this house is unchanged. The chest of drawers I helped pick out when I was ten still holds my baseball cards, grade school drawings, high school and college annuals. My first bike hangs in the garage. My brother's, too. The photographs of my mother and father—much younger than I ever knew them—still stand side by side, where they always have, on their dressing table. The yard is as neat, the evergreens as well trimmed as they were when I was a child.

My parents crafted and carved into everything here the hope that one of us one day would return to carry on in this house. That care dwells at the center of the regret I feel for having left Idaho, my parents, and this home, for having broken a connection my grandfather, nearly a hundred years ago, worked so hard to anchor. Living in a nation of broken connections is little solace; in this empty house my leaving feels a lot like betrayal.

My wife, my brother, and I begin peering into closets, sorting through boxes. Dad's clothes, his shoes, his hats, his rings are still in place. Mom hadn't touched them. Neither can I. Instead I fumble through her purse, running my fingers along the edges of her glasses, looking through the familiar names I find in her address book, then I put it all back and set the purse on the night stand—where it belongs.

FEBRUARY 28: No wonder I didn't recognize the Boise River the other day; its flooding fills the news. The river is pushing hard against city bridges, breaking apart walkways in sight of the State Capitol building, undermining levees. Down river, near Eagle, farmland is flooding. The *Idaho Statesman* says the source of all this water is a January thaw shoved hard against a record snowfall, and since the first of February, water managers have been forced to release a controlled flood from upstream reservoirs to make room for spring runoff. The paper warns that another string of hot days, or a bout of heavy rains, could transform the Boise into an "uncontrollable torrent." The city is at the mercy of the elements, it says, and the thought of the Boise eluding control, mustering a torrent, displaying a flash of wildness I'd assumed was long gone, makes me wonder what else I've missed about this river.

In the late morning my wife, my brother, and I meet with my parents' attorney. He explains the details of probate, state law, and all the other procedural nuances required to divide property. He asks if we plan to sell the house, and we all three respond with shrugs and silence. We know we must give it up—we have lives elsewhere, obligations, friends, and little choice—but none of us can yet say the words aloud.

We learn that the process will require time, and later my wife and I decide to stay in Boise for as long as it takes to settle things. She and I have more flexibility than my brother, who must return to his job in a few days; we're self-employed and can move what we must up here for now. I've wanted to spend more time in Idaho the older I've become, the magnetism of home growing stronger as the years pass, and although this is not the homecoming I would have chosen, it is certainly the one I've inherited.

I want to stay on until the loss sinks in, until a little more living dilutes the dying. I want to prune Mom's roses and weed the garden. I want to plant lobelia around the flowerbeds. I want to trim the hedges. I want to spend time following my parents' shadows through this house, through this town. Then, maybe, I can go.

FEBRUARY 29: My wife and I drive down Capitol Boulevard before dawn and stop near the river at Julia Davis Park. Water swirls high on the trunks of black cottonwoods; the current pushes, hissing; yet in a few spots the trees are dense enough to create a backwater. In the calm, mallards, wood ducks, and a pair of common mergansers paddle a flooded forest that looks more like the cypress swamps of Florida than the usually arid Boise Valley.

The sun appears on the horizon as a saffron thread of light, then loses itself in cloud. Silhouetted against that milky sky, last year's nests hover among bare branches like dark stars. How exposed, unadorned, and intricate winter can be. I'd almost forgotten. And there *is* color: in the yellow bark on a tangled cluster of twigs, in the beet-red buds on another, in the butter and cream of cattail fuzz, in the pale amber of dormant grasses. Colors as soft as whispers.

We spot red crossbills in a pine tree, prying seeds open with strong, sharp beaks. Canada geese trundle across a patch of open ground. A single great blue heron stands motionless and nearly invisible within a cluster of reeds, then cantilevers its ophidian neck out and strikes at something we cannot see.

I'm trying to refloat myself. As we walk the Greenbelt path along the river, I reclaim a little of Idaho with each step.

Yet as we cross under the Broadway Avenue Bridge, the riverbank reminds me that it too has not escaped change. On the opposite shore a restaurant, bar, and sprawling parking lot stand where once there was only a grassy field. On this side, office buildings crowd the river, blocking the sun along the path as pinstriped workers peer out from tinted windows. This complex, Park Center, was the first built in the river's floodplain as growth boomed in the seventies, and its approval opened the door for levee building, channel dredging, and floodplain encroachment along much of the Boise's course. Changes have so altered the river's topography that most recent maps of the floodplain are useless. No wonder, as we walk farther east into the exclusive River Run housing development—with its dredged lake, engineered channels, fabricated islands—I feel as if I've stumbled into someone else's Idaho.

MARCH 18: The sky is clear, with just a wisp of cloud. I've been working in the garden, reluctantly digging the last of the funereal flower arrangements into the ground for compost. The weather forecast predicts a high in the sixties and warns that three nights of above freezing temperatures in the mountains will increase the flood danger dramatically.

The *Idaho Statesman* is running a front page, five-part series on
the problem. Susan Stacy, former director of Boise's planning
department, is lecturing on the history of flood control
on the Boise River, and local bookstores prominently display her
book on the subject: *When the River Rises*. The conservation
group Idaho Rivers United has declared the Boise an endangered
waterway, due to the rapacious loss of floodplain to development,
and, on the evening news, owners of riverfront homes begin to ask
about flood insurance and sandbags.

MARCH 19: I'm alone in the house now. My wife has left to take
care of business back in California. To keep my mind off her
leaving, I work in the yard as the temperature rises to 80 degrees.
Yellow daffodils and blue crocuses have popped up everywhere.
Mom's roses are leafing out. The grass needs cutting. I spend the
afternoon poring through Dad's file on the sprinkler system, trying
to figure out how to turn it on, trying to decipher his scribbled
notes and diagrams. Once I've learned to distinguish master valve
from drainage valve I have water spraying the lawn as if I lived here.

MARCH 20: I drive to Barber Park at dawn, before the sun has
topped the hills north of town. Wearing a jacket stuffed with field
guides, I'm reacquainting myself to the Boise, my hometown river.

The weather has turned cool again, might even temper the
flooding, but the river looks humped up in the center and its
surface swirls. Northern flickers glide overhead, flashing red with
each beat of their wings. Wood ducks perch above. A pair of
kestrels peers down from a high branch. We study each other. I
pull out a field guide and compare the drawings to what I see
above, the black teardrops framing the eyes, the cinnamon breasts,
and the male's gunmetal wings. I find a mourning dove with twigs
in its beak, building a nest in a tangled thicket.

I've explored nearly the whole length of the river as it flows
through town, but I keep returning to this spot, to Barber Park,

and to the undeveloped woodland downstream. For ten to twenty minutes of quiet walking I am free of the changes that have swallowed my past and much of the river's floodplain. This side, the south side, is parkland. It is not pristine, it does not contain the wide expanse of black cottonwood forest Captain Benjamin Bonneville and his group of French explorers spotted in 1833, but it does sync with memory. These woods, and the open pastureland on the north side of the river, make up the largest undeveloped tract of land left in town. Here I find wildlife. Here I am free of the trophy homes, golf courses, and business parks that squeeze the rest of the river like a stranger's embrace.

There was none of that when I was growing up. The city greeted its namesake river like most cities of the time, with indifference, with overgrazed fields, gravel pits, and rendering plants. No one dreamed of living or working along its banks. Summer irrigation demands often dropped the river's flow to a fetid trickle, a river of mud and gravel. The Boise, the explanation went, was a working river.

In the seventies, things changed. A budding sense of civic pride and environmental consciousness came together in a plan for a system of parks and continuous public trails along the river. The Greenbelt was born. Over the next decade, the city purchased land and constructed paths, closed rendering plants, and transformed gravel pits into ponds; Boy Scouts planted trees; naturalists catalogued habitat; volunteers built nesting boxes. The result was a river park running through the heart of the city, a place where families as well as bald eagles could fish within sight of downtown office towers. The resurrection of the Boise drew national praise.

But public works created private opportunity. The *Wall Street Journal* declared the river clean up "a major spur to economic development" and soon planners were looking at the river as more than mere open space. As is the fundamental nature of rivers, the Boise spread out as it entered the valley, braiding itself into an unruly collection of channels that appeared to many as the antithesis of intelligent land use. With the coming of new Federal flood insurance policies (which had the unintended effect of encouraging floodplain development by removing much of the risk), and business pressure to promote growth downtown, the city allowed engineers to build levees and carve channels where the original park plan had never intended them to be. Development began pushing the river from both sides, replacing floodplain with real estate and ecological concern with economic. The river, it was thought, could be engineered into a placid backdrop to the good life.

MARCH 22: The sun is determined today. Tender new leaves drift like smoke through willow trees and high water has the city warning kayakers not to surf a large standing wave that has materialized on the west side of town. The river has pushed through an earthen dam at Logger's Creek and gobbled up a hundred feet of Greenbelt trail. "We're going to see a lot more of this before we're done," warns a Boise Parks and Recreation Department manager.

In the past the Boise River had forcefully, if infrequently, reclaimed its floodplain. The very land its namesake town now occupies was carved out by water that wandered the Boise valley eons ago. Once free of the mountains, flooding occurred along its 64-mile length, from the foothills, through towns and farmland, to its junction with the Snake River, near Parma. The *Idaho Statesman* has run colored maps and charts showing that, in the Boise area alone, a 100-year flood would affect an estimated 5,000 to 10,000 people living next to the river. A 500-year flood would spill far from the river's edge, engulfing much of downtown Boise and an inestimable number of people. The paper fails to mention that in 1863, observers described a flood that spread from "bluff to bluff," covering the entire width of the valley and carrying a flow estimated at *fifteen times* that running today.

⌐ ⌐ ⌐

Last night I went to dinner with an old friend. He and I were close in college, close like you can be only in college, that kind of closeness that feels eternal, yet quickly dissipates with time and distance. We went our separate ways soon after graduation. While I moved from Boise to more school, to New York and Los Angeles and then a small town on the central Californian coast, he stayed close to home, wandered the Northwest, working as a carpenter and a contractor at a time when those jobs were scarce. His dreams were slow to emerge. He struggled. When we first said hello, I could see it in his eyes.

But he was quick to point out that his fortune had turned. He had landed a job with one of the big developers in town and was soon talking breathlessly of the growth taking place, of the booming local economy, of prices per square foot, of economies of scale, and as he talked his hands began to trace the air, filling the space with blueprints, spreadsheets, and plats of undeveloped land. His eyes gleamed like a raptor's. The Boise Valley *owed* him he said. He had back wages coming and it was easy to see he'd use a backhoe, a bulldozer, or anything else to get at them. It was also easy to see the common ground we once shared crumble away.

I tried jumping to less acquisitive subjects. I asked about his wife and his aging mother. I told him of my mother's death and my hesitation to sell the house. But when I told him of the time I'd spent at the river, it only reminded him of a proposed thirty-five-hundred-home development planned to break ground on the last open riverfront land in Boise—the land across the river from where I'd been spending my time. The thought horrified me, and I told him so.

He leaned forward, flashing the kind of paternal smile an old sage offers a student whose naivete runs far deeper than words can wash away. He pushed aside his plate. He drew the Boise River across the table with a stroke of his finger, then drew in the levees he would build to give a healthy portion of those thirty-five hundred homes a riverfront view. "It's inevitable," he said with a satisfied shrug, "as natural, as undeniable as water over rock."

As my friend's conviction grew, mine faltered. I made a few feeble remarks about the value of tradition, of land preservation, but this old friend spit the words back at me like chunks of bad fruit. He leaned forward, pointed a finger at my chest, and said, "Look," the last shred of patience gone from his voice, "you've *always* wanted Idaho to be your little refuge, some kind of secret hideout frozen in time, a place you could come back to whenever you needed it, whenever you'd had enough of the rest of your world. But you'd never expected the world to find Idaho first, had you?"

He was right. I slumped in my chair. He had aimed for my heart and found it.

APRIL 3: The realtor's assistant came by this morning. He walked through the house, measuring rooms, taking photographs. He talked of selling strategies, timing, and when he pushed more forms toward me, I signed them. As rain slid down the living room window, he pounded a "For Sale" sign into soft ground.

Afterward, I planned to begin packing up my parents' belongings. I started with the basement, but my father's first saddle, a seventy-year-old Sears and Roebuck complete with angora chaps, confounded me, as did the shelves upon shelves of my mother's dill pickles (deliciously crisp ones for which she had always promised, but never given me a recipe). I uncovered a box of their letters, gave up on the packing and instead sat on the cold cement floor reading through the afternoon. When my wife called asking when I'd be home, I told her I wasn't sure, so much to do....

APRIL 6: I'm stuck; I've stalled. I can't bear to even think about dismantling this house. Instead, I read about water and rivers. I've gathered books on the subject and find a cool sanctuary in the language of fluid dynamics, immersing myself in the clear syntax of liquid motion. I've stacked hardbacks on the kitchen table like sandbags along the river, forming a bookish wall between me and leaving.

I've learned that water is the strangest thing. Scientists who study it pepper their descriptions with words such as *peculiar, abnormal,* and *freakish.* They ponder what properties in water allow it to flow in rivers, freeze in quiet backwaters, and then drift into the sky to form clouds; why it becomes denser as a liquid than as a solid; and how it can dissolve and carry away almost anything it touches. It shouldn't behave that way.

Water seems bent to the needs of life, and maybe that is why the Boise River attracts me now, why I feel such an inexplicable empathy with the flooding. The granitic upthrust of a mountain range is far too slow to register on human senses, the searing crack of a lightning strike far too swift, but tumbling water holds motion that feels somehow knowable. Something in the clarity of river current on a day shot with sunlight and its stunning opacity on one dense with cloud seems to offer everything and nothing at all. I can't help but think that to grasp even a drop of what force moves water is to hold meanings very near to the core of what moves us all.

And if water is a wonder, I've learned, a river is the rarest of its expressions: at any given moment, only 3 percent of the earth's water is free of an ocean's grasp, three-quarters of that is tightly held in glaciers and polar ice sheets, and most of the rest is sunk deep underground. An infinitesimal dribble, a mere 0.036 percent inhabits the world's lakes, streams, and rivers. The Boise River, as modest as it may appear, is by nature a singularity.

APRIL 7: I sit near the curve of a wide meander, a "trouble spot" the paper says, marked by a pile of sandbags and slumping ground. As the river swings through its arc, the water on the far shore, on the inside curve, slows. It has less distance to travel, and no longer having the velocity to hold the sediment it carries, releases it. I can see a sandy beach emerging from the murky current there. On my side the river is "hungry," speeding up as it runs along the outside turn, consuming more sediment, eating away at the soft soil at my feet like the blade of a circular saw. The entire river is moving toward me, deepening this meander in response to high water. This, I've learned, is how a river balances its energies, adjusts to rains, runoff, topography, and all the rest. It's what a river does. As sediments are both dropped and washed away, the river bends, wriggles, becomes animate.

As I've read, I've begun to sense that the dry language of hydrology—a discipline filled with phrases like *velocity profiles* and *supercritical laminars, hydraulic drops* and *jumps, viscous sublayers* and *flow separation*—is an oddly bloodless patois for describing a process that sounds very close to the movement of a living thing. I've begun to sense magic behind the motion. The more I read about rivers the more I imagine an ancient, sentient being lurking in the Boise, lurking beneath this skin of muddy water.

I look across the river to the land where the developers hope to build. I try to imagine a forest of houses where I've only seen a few cottonwoods and perching osprey. I watch small slabs of soil break away from that bank, like the calving of a miniature glacier. They remind me that the subject of change is not a simple one, nor is it divided only, as my old friend believes, between those clinging to the past and those bulldozing into the future. This river is not simply *place,* a static channel conveying water, but *process,* and its unrelenting flood an elegant lesson in change. Building homes and businesses on a floodplain is as pure a denial of that change as anything of which I could be accused. Developers often spread the banner of change while denying it with rebar and riprap, building on ocean cliffs and inland gorges, on barrier islands and active faults. My friend and I have both of us cobbled together levees on the soft shores of our own illusions: he tricked by the seemingly inanimate nature of rivers, I by life itself, and both by movement just slow enough that we mistook it for solid ground. Yet the Boise has, for over two months now, been a reminder that rivers and lives are only slightly more static than clouds in the sky, that Creation *is* a work in progress.

APRIL 8: In the afternoon I drive to Barber Park. The sun is bright, the sky deep blue. As I walk west, through the corkscrew song of red-winged blackbirds, I catch a fragrance I can't quite place. It has a hint of summer in it. I scan the ground for open flowers, but see none. I search the trees for blossoms. I pull a cottonwood branch toward me, its leaves folded tightly within resin-coated buds, and touch one to the tip of my finger. I bring the amber resin to my nose and suddenly:

It is deep summer and the night sizzles with heat and I am riding my bicycle along the banks of the Boise River, sliding through eddies of sweet riverine air that have my skin tingling and I am riding fast, my hands folded in my lap, the town still small enough, its lights still few enough, that on the water's surface, I glimpse the Milky Way.

River memories tumble through my head.

A bee has stung my brother and his face is swollen, dark red, and he is gasping for breath. I am eleven today and watching my father scoop up his limp body and run for the car, and as I stand ankle deep in river water, a slice of cake in my hand, I want nothing more from this birthday than to see them both again.

I am older and swimming toward shore, my thin arms burn with fatigue, but I am too shy to call for help and I am imagining, for the first time, my own dying.

The memories fall.

My mother is young and beautiful and my hand is hidden completely within the soft folds of her own and we are slipping our bare feet into the river and its cold makes us squeal. Her eyes are bright. She is laughing. Her hair is filled with light.

I settle onto a log and stare into water, into a river that has spoken even when I haven't listened. A cliff swallow glides past, inches from the water's surface. Then another and another. Like me, they are neither locals nor newcomers, and it feels good to be in their company, good to be reminded that we are all, in the deepest sense, transients. Even the water that flows at my feet is on its way to somewhere else. Yet, I come from this river valley; this ground holds my family's bones, and it will bind me to this place forever. I stare into the water and it is full of reflections, of trees and circling osprey, of memories, of hills and home.

～ ～ ～

It is not characteristic of my clan to ascribe transcendental properties to rivers. After all, I come from a stolid line of Western pragmatists, clear-eyed skeptics, and hardscrabble farmers, too thinly sheltered from the elements to embellish them with what they would see as untethered mysticism. The call of Manifest Destiny still rings in their ears. My father, for one, would never have called a river anything but a river, yet there is no denying I caught a look in his eyes on the Boise that betrayed a certain kind of wonder. He had no words for that wonder, but it was surely there.

I've had to look to other cultures for those words. The Inuits, for example, believe that the world once ran with rivers flowing both uphill and down; but Raven, the creator, thought the arrangement made life too easy for people and forced all rivers to flow downhill. Many refused to acknowledge the change and fought the current from then on. But the Inuits called those who understood, those who could hear voices in the water and recognize the language spoken, River People. River People learned to use the current without resisting its flow.

And the river never surprised them when it washed away time, familiar places, and the people they loved. They knew that one day a great flood would gather them up as well, a flood not only flowing downhill, but always, inexorably home.

I look at my watch; I see that it is nearly six o'clock and the sun is still warm and two hours from the horizon, and the riverbank glows in a way that seems to shout *Yes!* there are moments that come free, where the world is generous and overflowing. I look up and every budding branch on every cottonwood tree is golden.

The Shadowy St. Joe

Debra Hieronymus

Out from its headwaters, in the Bitterroot Mountains that divide Idaho and Montana, the St. Joe River lunges over rocks and around logs, plunges through narrow channels and winds in rugged curves that will eventually straighten and slow as the current flows into the marshlands at the edge of Lake Coeur d'Alene. Over the centuries, it seems as though two rivers have formed—one turbulent and stormy, rising in spring thaw and gnawing at its levees, the other gentle and calm—and shaped these craggy hillsides and riverbanks.

In early September spiral tufts of cottonwood float in the St. Joe's clear current. Aspen, willow, and white alder stain the far bank with russet, vermillion, ruby, and yellow, and on the mountain slopes beyond the ruffling water, tamaracks spot the high timber country with burnished hues as their needles turn to rust.

On such a September afternoon in 1970, my father stood in shallow water at an oxbow, his Levis and olive work shirt dark against the brilliance of the leaves. A thin man, long waisted, his six-foot frame was betrayed by short legs reduced even further by the water's distortion. A slight breeze ruffled his hair as he wove quick patterns of line, creating an illusion of a mayfly, an illusion he hoped a rainbow or cutthroat would strike.

A few feet behind him on the river's smoothed rocks, I sat resting my chin on my doorknob knees. "Skinny as a ragged tomcat," he often said. Long hair, the same brown as my father's, wisped about my face. Shivering, I wished I had brought jeans or a blanket. My shorts, as my father had warned me that afternoon, weren't enough in the cooling day. I rocked, hugging my legs, trying to warm my body. Three months earlier, I had turned twelve, an age where I began to discover how I wanted my relationship with my father to be, and how it truly was.

⌒ ⌒ ⌒

As we had driven the ten miles or so upriver from our home in St. Maries, Idaho, my father had told me that once he found a spot to fish, I couldn't move; I might scare potential supper.

I sat tight.

On the far shore, a tan spot moved. A deer, a skittish whitetail or more likely a mule deer, nibbled on serviceberry or purple heather in the thicket of Englemann spruce and lodgepole. I imagined following the deer, swimming the narrow swath, shaking away the wet, and twirling among the trees. My body grew warm. I made a pallet from fallen pine needles and napped.

"Come on, it's time to go."

Dad shook my shoulder. Sleep pains numbing my limbs, I crawled to my feet and rubbed my tender calves. I longed to go back to sleep, but the sight of rainbow trout on his stringer transfixed me. He held them up for me to see. Underwater, they had flashed with the colors that gave them their name—primary, bright—but in the late afternoon sun they dulled and grayed, and their rainbows disappeared.

"Nice ones, eh?"

One of the trout flopped, gulped air, fought eventual death. Scales slimy and slick. The smell, well, *fishy*. Not what I expected. The pictures painted under the wavering water didn't match their scent or texture. I wrinkled up my nose and rubbed my hand on my shorts, trying to wipe away the feel.

"Yuck."

I climbed into the pickup.

The sun grazed the mountaintops, haloed the valley in soft evening light, lavender, rose and ocher, a paling light that followed our descent into town.

Across the dark cab, I looked at my father's profile. His nose was the only mark of his Choctaw heritage. Not large, but broad, rounded.

"Dad, will you teach me to fly-fish?"

He snorted. "Girls can't handle fly-fishing. A bobber and spinning reel would be more to your liking. Fly-fishing is a man's sport."

⌒ ⌒ ⌒

Today I take Highway 95 up the steep grade of the Lewiston Hill, out of the pulp-mill smell of the valley, and into the Palouse's hills sown with peas and lentils. After I have driven through Moscow, where, at the age of forty, I've been taking graduate classes at the University of Idaho for the past month, the landscape begins to change. Past the northern city limits, the hills roll into low mountains. Douglas fir and white pine are closer to the highway now; the occasional field of barley or wheat presses in. It's a road I know well, and I don't pay much attention, but listen to NPR until the signal becomes a whisper. I'm thinking about my father's phone call last night, the phone call that is bringing me back to St. Maries, where I grew up. Come up the river, he'd said, I'd know where to find him.

Up Skyline Pass. More fields, then the town of Tensed on the Coeur d'Alene Indian Reservation, then Plummer, fifty-one miles north of Moscow. I turn right on Highway 5. Eighteen more miles. Turning, twisting miles down PeeDee Hill, past Lake Chacolet, Hidden Lake, Rocky Point, and Benewah Lake—the chain lakes that link into Lake Coeur d'Alene.

Before I reach Benewah Lake, I pull over at Rocky Point in Heyburn State Park to savor the moment of my return. Heyburn, as I had learned from my father, is the first state park in the Pacific Northwest, and, created in 1908, one of the oldest in the nation. Farther down the road, a trestle covers a portion of the marsh at the edge of the lake where I used to fish from a boat rowed under the scaffolding or from the bridge, leaning over to hook northern pike or largemouth bass (I used to call them Bigmouth fish when I was younger.) Sometimes I would see a heron or osprey behind the screen of brush, a dusky blue shape like an apparition that I had to look at twice.

Finally I pull out of the parking lot and drive north.

I get my first glimpse of the St. Joe as it channels into Benewah Lake. My father once told me that the Joe is the highest navigable river in the United States. I am not sure what the *highest navigable river* means; I have never asked. Perhaps today, when I see him, I will ask: Does it mean sailing ships can navigate the river? Or does it mean that the Joe is the highest river, elevation-wise, that can be navigated?

And why haven't I asked?

But I really don't see the river; what I actually see are the banks marked by multicolored broadleaf cutting through the surface of the lake. The St. Joe is hiding behind its banks, an apparition as dusky blue as any heron or osprey.

I keep driving up the northern region of Idaho's panhandle until I come to St. Maries, population 2,600, mostly mill workers and loggers, a few shopkeepers, and a few wealthy newcomers who have settled here for tranquility. The air feels different here at 2,200 feet; my senses awaken.

The sun begins to curve behind me as I enter town from the west, past the service station with its diesel pumps set up for truck drivers hauling chips or logs 110 miles down to the lumber mill in Lewiston. I follow Main Street (Highway 5) past the brick-layered taverns, their doors flung open in this Indian summer heat, their early afternoon patrons sipping beer. Craner's Grocery has been torn down. It was a Mom-and-Pop operation where my school bus driver occasionally stopped, especially toward the end of May when the sun was blazing and the kids cranky, and bought his fares Popsicles or Cokes.

At the junction past the bridge, past Eddy's Service Station and Car Wash, I have a choice. I could continue left on Highway 3 to Coeur d'Alene and abandon this, my search for my father, or I can turn right and drive upriver where the calm water turns shallow and swift, where I know he will be.

To the left is the old swimming hole in its thicket of brush and weeds. My best friend's family had built a small dock and hung a tire swing from one of the ancient cottonwoods that crowded the banks with their roots uncovered on bare ground. The leaves were so dense that, to get warm enough for a swim, I had to lie on the dock until I couldn't bear the heat. Then I would unwind the rope, plant my feet on the tire and swing out as far as possible. Sometimes it took three or four swings before I had courage to let go. I would hit freezing water and open my eyes under the murk where underwater plants waved with the roll of my splash and sticks brushed my legs. And then some *thing* would brush my leg and I would force myself up, up, up until I burst through the water's curtain into the leaf-spattered day. Floating on my back, paddling with my legs, I would return to shore.

Those days are long gone.

I turn right at the sign marking the St. Joe River Road.

A mown field is on the left, a sprinkling of houses on the right, then a dirt road leading to the new high school, set halfway up St. Maries Mountain.

I had attended the old high school, built in 1913, where plaster ceilings chunked into beakers and onto notebooks. Its dim, dank halls, lined with dusty lockers, had left only enough room for two backpacked students to move without difficulty. It had been torn down the year after I graduated, 1975.

⌒ ⌒ ⌒

As I travel upriver, I think of my father weaving his line above the current, his eyes narrow against sunlight, his face and body an orchestrated movement as he casts again and again, teasing trout until one runs with his homespun fly.

The mountain overhangs the highway, throwing the asphalt into shadow-splashed patterns. Soon the road abandons the river's course, cuts across an open field that stretches between road and water where nodding lily pads circle a pond's rim.

Another mile or so and Thomas Creek spills into the Joe. I pull off onto a graveled access, which gives way to a fenced pasture. A roan gelding roams the dried-up grassland, stopping now and then to relish the few green stalks that have survived August's glare.

Hot, I climb out of the car, stretch, pull the wire loop off the gate's post and walk the river's dike. The gelding trots toward me. I run my hand down his warm neck, feel the heat rise from his hide. My face buried in his blond mane, I take in the horseflesh aroma, the animalness of him. He moves away from me and grazes on stalks.

Across the pasture and up the highway, two dirt roads diverge and lead to four lots for four mobile homes. Two on the lower road, two on the upper. It's the place I called home as a teen. We lived in a trailer on the uppermost lot, the lot that looked out over the highway and the pasture. The trailer is gone, in its place a prefabricated house.

As a girl of twelve, I often would cross the highway to the field, where a restless horse pastured. His massive muscles rippled with every movement, even standing still and swatting at flies with his tail, and my imagination wrought images of the him standing on his hind legs, his front hooves batting the air, his whinny a high-pitched scream. I imagined running from him, my legs pumping, afraid to look back lest I be trampled. Sometimes in imagination I tripped, and the horse pawed at me with those huge hooves until I became unconscious.

To overcome my fear, I tried to befriend him with offerings of carrots or apples. At first, I couldn't bring myself to go up to him and feed him by hand. The horse would begin to move toward me, neighing, and I would drop my offering and rush to the gate.

But I would watch him from behind the safety of the fence, watch as his solid body moved with a self-assuredness that I longed to possess. Gradually I began to move a few feet closer and closer to him. Before I became completely aware of what I was doing, the horse was taking sugar cubes from my palm. And even though my fear faded, I still felt the shiver of the unknown each time I approached him.

That shiver of the unknown was also what I felt for my father. There were times when his impatience with me would grow into anger. He yelled at me for not hanging up my clothes or clearing the dishes right after dinner, told me I had to learn to respect his rules or get another whipping with his hand or his leather belt. And although he treated my younger brother and sister the same way, I often took the brunt of his anger toward them. Spankings meant for them became my own.

If, during the day while my father worked, I committed some act that would not set right with him, I would escape to the pasture. Sometimes I would take a halter I had made from a piece of rope and sling it about the horse's head. Leading him along the dike, I would tell him of my dreams, my hopes, my plans for the future. I also told him how I wished my father would love me for who I was and not for who he wanted me to be. Or, if I could only be perfect, then perhaps my father would see the good in me.

I tried my hardest to please my father in the smallest ways: bringing him coffee, the paper, turning the television to his favorite program. I studied hard in school, attaining A's and B's. But his anger rose time and time again. Nothing I did kept away my father's irritation.

And as I look back now, I can see that my father wasn't particularly angry with me, but at the circumstances surrounding his life. He had left a good job in Oklahoma to come back home to Idaho, to log in the woods as he did as a teen, woods that he had often talked about with a faraway look as we had sat around the dining table in our ranch-style house in Muskogee. To work in the woods meant relying on the weather, which was as unstable as the price of lumber in the 1970s, and unemployment ran high for woodsmen in spring thaw, blazing summer days, and freezing winters. Dad worked when he could and collected unemployment insurance when he could not.

But if I could find some connection between my father and myself, then, perhaps his rage would soften and we could become friends. Fishing, I hoped, would become a way for me to bond with my father, a common link between us. And sure enough, even though he would not teach me to fly-fish, he did teach me to fish with a rod and reel, with a bobber and a worm for bait, threaded on a single hook.

⌒ ⌒ ⌒

The day he taught me to fish was shortly after our expedition up the St. Joe.

At the rim of our yard, my father and I stood above the crumbling ledge, a vertical wall of dug-out land, a man-made dirt and rock cliff. He taught me to cast off the rim, showing me how to release the Zebco's button just at the right moment so that the line with its light lead near the single hook arched over my head and across the precipice. And a week or so later, after my father had taught me how to remove fish from the hook without getting stung by a fin, I tried out my new skill on my own.

Damp ground. A mass of worms wiggled, trying to squeeze out of my reach. I squatted with the coffee can by my side, capturing bait. Worm juice mingled with dirt, stained my fingers, turned my nails into dark crescents. Finally I slid down the steep path with my pole flung over my shoulder, the stringer looped about my waist, and the brimming coffee can gripped in my fingers. Now I could catch fish, just as my father did, and I would be able to befriend him in the same way I had the horse. I crossed the marshy field to the shore of the Joe, climbed onto a protruding granite slab under which fish liked to settle, and set up camp. Baiting the hook like he taught me—worm stabbed in the middle, then threaded—I tossed the line, watched the bobber, waited for any movement, any play.

This fishing, this sitting, was passive. I longed to whip a line above water, longed to wade in knee-deep current, working a fly-fishing rod with the same ease as my father. I daydreamed as I fished the Joe, the same river he took trout from—at least we had that in common—and I imagined that the river's current would connect us. I watched myself take my place beside my father, showing him that I was capable of controlling the line the way he controlled the action of a fly.

But he had told me again and again that fly-fishing is an intricate sport, that I wouldn't enjoy the time it took to learn the technique, that deep-water fishing would be more to my liking.

The red-and-white plastic ball submerged. I jerked the rod and reeled in my first perch. Dad would be proud, would congratulate me on my catch. Soon I had a mess, enough for dinner. Fish rolled in flour and cornmeal, fried in lard until crisp, golden brown; thick-sliced potatoes to follow in the same fashion, cooked in the remaining fish-sweetened grease; garden tomatoes, black-eyed peas, fresh rings of yellow onion, white bread, and sugared iced tea.

When I took home my stringer of fish and held them up for my father to see, he only grunted. "There's a lot of little ones there, Deb, but enough for supper. Your brother will fillet them for dinner tonight."

My smile vanished. I walked away, thinking that at least my fish would taste better than the brown meat of a trout.

⌐ ⌐ ⌐

This afternoon I crawl on top of a mica-flecked boulder, warm from sun. The house, where once our trailer had stood, shines with the downing sun. A breeze ruffles my graying shoulder-length hair. I still have not learned to fly-fish.

Unleashed leaves drift, swirl, ride the river. One larger than my hand floats the air and lands on the rock beside me. I trace the veins of the orange-kissed yellow leaf, as pliant as my fingers. The leaf stashed in my shorts' back pocket, I double-check the wire loop on the gate and drive up the river road.

Stainless air seeps through the car vents, through my open window. A crow caws, glides through late afternoon sunlight with his wings spread. I cross a steel-girded bridge where a waterfall cascades over mossy rocks and forms a deep pool before funneling under the bridge to the river.

Wading in that pool, trying to catch crawdads, sliding on the slick stones, losing balance, splashing into waist-deep water, stirring sediment—how clearly I remember a young girl's pleasure as the day turned salmon and silver-platter blue.

Around a hairpin corner, the mountains free the highway. The terrain is more rugged, the pitch of the mountain steeper; and the roots of the trees claw the dirt as though a shift in wind could blow them down. I cross another bridge where the river, narrowing, tumbles on my right. I imagine cutthroat and Dolly Varden trout fighting the swift water or hiding beneath overhanging rock and broken branches with leaves like dozens of fingers running their tips against the river's motion.

I could drive another 102 miles south on Highway 50 until I come to St. Regis, Montana. Instead, I take a left across a fledgling bridge and follow a strip of road honed from the mountainside that goes up Fishhook Creek. The creek bends, straightens, rounds another bend, flows into the river. My father's grubby pickup is parked under a white aspen, in the bit of shade its last leaves afford. I shut off my car and roll to a stop.

My father stands in a deep pocket, a slow eddy, where the whirling water laps his thighs. He was never one for wearing suspender-hooked waders, said if he fell, he'd bottom out with the water weight. Through my bug-speckled windshield, I lose the image of my father as a young man and notice for the first time how his thinning hair has grayed at the temples. His cheeks are sunburned, ruddy; he still refuses to wear a cap. He's put on pounds, his belly hides a belt buckle, but he still moves with a fly-fisherman's grace. As he flicks the tip of his rod in a sidearm cast, his wrist is liquid and seamless.

The fly, probably a nymph, rafts the air. Candy-cane loops of line waver above the gentle curl of the water. Spruce, pine and aspen press the creekbed, throw elongated hints of themselves across the charging water while he stands in the fading sun, casting toward shadow.

I imagine easing the car door open and walking toward him. His back will still be turned as he tosses another cast, works the fly, and moves with the line's arc. The fly will float the ripples, hide as the water folds and refolds upon itself, transparent as new glass as it runs toward the river. Dusk will play on the tucks and pleats of the current, clean and cold as the first day I waded the St. Joe, pretending to toss my own line toward my own slow pocket to hook a cutthroat and watch as the trout rises toward light, curling his body as the river curls over itself, drops of water streaming off his sides. The trout hangs in the air, plunges to deep water, weaves through rocks and waterlogged brushwood, thrashes free and hides in shadows.

And I will ease into the cold water, my canvas boat shoes a cushion against the pebbled creekbed, the cold water soaking through the fabric, chilling my feet. My father will turn to face me, tuck his line next to his pole, and say, "Get out of the water, you'll catch your death."

But I will smile and open my arms.

His blue eyes will crinkle. As we hug, I will say, "I've come for my fly-fishing lesson, Dad."

And he will grin, then chuckle, shake his head with acceptance, and hand me the pole.

Hiking the Selway at Night

William Johnson

I wake in a fit of shivering. I'm lying in the bed of my small pickup, scrunched as far as I can get into my sleeping bag. Lined with cotton instead of Gore-Tex or down, the bag is no match for September in the Idaho Bitterroots. Even here, in the lower canyon of the Selway River, frost has emblazoned the evergreens. I nestle and squirm in the bag, pull the lip up over my head, but it's no use. If I don't move, and very soon, I'll risk getting hypothermic. I rise, put on my boots, chew a fruit-bar for calories, and begin walking vigorously around the truck, hugging myself to get warm. I'm surprised to see my watch reads 3:00 A.M. Hours ago, though it feels like only minutes now, an owl was calling from the nearby trees. I dozed off listening, and waking now in the cold, I feel a sense of dislocation, a rent in time.

The sky is a collage of blue, black, and purple, scatter-gunned by stars. To the east Venus hangs like a pendant, but the cold prevents me from star-gazing for long. My plan had been to camp overnight at the trailhead, rise for an early hike upriver, and spend the day fishing my way back. But I hadn't counted on the night turning so cold.

I consider cranking up the truck and turning the heater on, but reject the idea, eager to be on my way. On an impulse, I decide I'll use my small flashlight and begin hiking in the dark. This way I'll get even farther upstream than I'd planned. I put on my fishing vest, pack snacks and a lunch in my rucksack, assemble my fly rod, and, switching on the thin pencil-sized light, make my way to the sign that reads Selway River Trail. I feel clumsy and alien, although the flashlight casts a small halo of comfort on the cold ground, and I walk surrounded by a vast and utter darkness.

The trail is rocky and uneven. I grope for my way, stumbling over exposed roots or a sudden upstart boulder. The least sound startles me. A snapping twig sounds like a gunshot. When something—a cone or dead limb—drops from overhead, I feel I'm hearing the footfall of an animal in the nearby woods. Somewhere to my right moves the river, a heavy windlike rushing. And there's another sound, muffled and dragging, as if the current bears a slow lumbering downbeat. It seems to mingle with the knocking of my pulse, and it dawns on me: stones loosened by the current are wedging themselves against each other as they move. I'm listening to the dreamwork of the river.

I had thought the woods would be utterly silent. Instead, silence contains another field of sound, subtler and less predictable than the one I'm used to—the skirl of traffic, the ringing of an alarm clock, or random human chatter. I feel hyperactively alert, as if my senses have been rudely awakened. In the absence of vision and its illusion of reliable perspective, my smell and touch seem acute. Even in the cold, I can smell the smudgelike odor of duff and dead weeds, the punk of cottonwood and riverrot.

My plan to use the flashlight is working, but a second or two after the thought occurs to me, the dim beam falters and goes out. Certain I had replaced the batteries, I curse and fumble with the switch. But it's no use: the light is dead. Swallowed in darkness, I can barely see my fingers held inches from my face.

The shock sets in gradually. My thoughts stagger and accumulate, only to impress me with their uselessness. I slip off my pack, prop the fly rod on a ghostly bush, and sit down on a sloped bank of the trail. I think of hikes I've taken here with my daughter and one of my sons, but the images quickly fade. Flitting among them come images more disturbing—a bear lumbering up the trail; a cougar prowling the woods behind me. Habits of Zen practice come to the forefront of my mind. I sit still and focus on my breathing, letting thoughts come and go as they will, trying not to cling, then trying not to try.

☞ ☞ ☞

On a warm spring morning, my son and I are hiking upriver. He spots a family of mergansers paddling upstream. "Dad, are they ducks?" he asks me. I notice the sudden, supple readiness of his body as he watches them, the way his fine blond hair turns almost translucent in sunlight.

Night sweeps him away.

I give myself to my breathing.

He floats back again.

Now we are watching three otters swimming in midcurrent. He's excited and can't stop gesturing and pointing. One otter somersaults onto its back and throws us a quizzical look. Its expression troubles me. Neutral, yet cautioning, it says we're intruders, strangers who don't belong.

☞ ☞ ☞

Maybe only minutes have lapsed; maybe an hour, or more. I can see very little. Held close, my fingers look like stubs of wax. A ghostly bush won't befriend me. Neither will the vague lumped shapes near the path—are they boulders? The river is giving off mist, or so I assume, since I can see no stars overhead. From an indeterminate distance, raised, as if it hovers over the far bank of the river, a thin shaft of light leans down. I inventory the possible explanations: a stray moonbeam, a first crease of dawn, or more desperately, from the realm of the absurd, the tractor-beam of a

UFO. But there isn't a moon, and dawn is at least two hours away. The "beam" just hangs there, a dim elongated glow, barely distinguishable from the darkness around it.

There's no evidence the sky has lightened, but the next time I glance up, I *see* what I've been looking at. It's the trunk of a dead tree leaning from the *near* bank outward. Old and bleached, it looks like the dull beam of a flashlight seen through fog. Either my eyes have adjusted or dawn is approaching. Still, the tree seems strangely bodiless, a dim shaft of light connected to nothing, hanging in a vacuum of darkness.

In its general diffusion, the sound of the river has deceived me. What before was a rush and murmur is now dimly moving, about ten yards from where I sit. It could be a shimmering blanket of mist or a herd of ermine running in a foggy treadmill. It's still too dark for hiking, but thanks to my half-hour walk and the calmness induced by my attention to breathing, I've gotten warmer.

⌒ ⌒ ⌒

Clutching the tail of my shirt, my daughter tags behind me. Moments ago, we startled a young rattlesnake that was sunning near the trail. Its chirr of warning frightened her, and now she scolds me for having brought her into harm's way. I humor her, my head swimming in the delirium of snake-sound: beads shaking in a paper jar; the bearings of an old hand lawn mower run downhill.

I'm glad we've seen a Selway rattler, but I wish my daughter could overcome her fear and get more curious about what's around us. Or rather, I wish I could help her do that. But she's urgent that we keep moving, and though I've assured her I'll be on the lookout for snakes, I see that what she needs now is my indulgence, not my counseling. She tightens her grip, and we stumble along in a clumsy train.

It's high summer.

Beside us the river sparkles blue in sunlight.

⋐ ⋐ ⋐

Over the tops of the trees the sky looks like a velvet pincushion. I make out tall trunks etched against shades of blackish gray, but it's still too dark for hiking. The night woods goads my imagination with stories of former inhabitants or passers-through. A few years before, a friend who was hiking upstream near Moose Creek Ranger Station thought he was alone. He was surprised when a man wearing only a loincloth and carrying a bow and arrow bounded out of the brush. The fellow said he was seeking a "wilderness experience" and believed clothing and a pack would only spoil it. I imagine others haunting these woods at night, shady characters like Bill Moreland, the "ridgerunner," who, during the 1940s and '50s, lived as a vagabond and fugitive, stealing food from campers and ranchers, before fleeing again to the wilderness.

And I think, too, of ghosts. In June of 1979, a photographer from the *Spokesman-Review* was hiking with a friend below the Selway Lodge, a small private holding in the heart of the wilderness. Suddenly, a plane roaring over the canyon dropped one of its engines. The photographer took a shot of the flaming engine as it fell. Minutes later, after a second engine feathered out, the plane, a D-C 3, lurched into a crash dive. It came in low, snapped off the crown of a tall tree, flipped and plunged down into Wolf Creek Rapids, killing twelve of the fourteen forest-service workers aboard. The grim business of salvaging the wreckage went on for several days.

Three years after this tragedy, two members of a float-party drowned when their raft overturned in one of the Selway's rapids. Like the rugged country it drains, this wild river can be treacherous.

I close my eyes.

Fragments of shining metal glimmer, then drift away.

In the river a trickle of blood dissolves.

⌒ ⌒ ⌒

From Hidden Lake in North Central Idaho's Salmon River Range, the headwaters of the Selway gather to creek-sized strength, tumbling twenty-five miles to Magruder Guard Station on the Nez Perce Trail Road. This road is the boundary between the River of No Return and the Selway-Bitterroot wilderness, combined areas about the size of New Hampshire. From Magruder, full-fledged now, the river flows north, meandering through canyons toward the mouth of Moose Creek, where it swings west in a run to Selway Falls, having cut through a patchwork of granite peaks, ridges, saddles, and glacial cirques that form the rugged west slope of the Idaho Rockies.

As a designated Wild and Scenic River, Idaho's upper Selway is protected from development. Provisions of the Wilderness Act of 1964 keep its watershed from being roaded, mined or logged. The lower roaded stretch, where I've often camped with my family, is noted for its calm clear pools and tranquil current. *Sal-wah* may be a mingling of Nez Perce and Shoshoni words, meaning, roughly, "good canoe water," or "sound of water flowing." Whatever the case, when I hear the name, it is where I want to be. But here in the dark, those quiet lower stretches seem far away.

Slowly my mental map of the river dissolves. My mind is a miasma of cold air, damp smells, and river-sound. I want badly to walk again, but I'm torn by conflicting impulses. I want to take in as much of the rugged canyon as I can. I also want simply to *be*, and embrace whatever presents itself, which just now is the dark.

Or is it? Have those grayish lumps that loom along the trail become boulders? If I'm careful, I can see just enough to make my way. A year from now, reading Peter Matthiessen's *Snow Leopard*, which recounts a six-month trek through the high ranges of Nepal and Tibet, I will relive my night on the river. Matthiessen cites an expert on Tantric meditation-walking:

> The walker must neither speak, nor look from side to
> side. He must keep his eyes fixed on a single distant

object and never allow his attention to be attracted by anything else. When the trance has been reached, though normal consciousness is for the greater part suppressed, it remains sufficiently alive to keep the man aware of the obstacles in his way, and mindful of his direction and goal.

Matthiessen met several such walkers who negotiated steep trails in high mountain passes. There are well-authenticated stories of their being able to walk this way in the dark. Though I've practiced Zen meditation, I think better of walking "blind." Still, Matthiessen makes me wonder how far meditative practice might take us. Maybe the Buddhists are right: thinking gets in the way of our becoming attuned to the emptiness of Being. If I could suspend thinking and trust my immediate intuition, would a deeper connecting center rise to guide me?

I can make out shades of gray beyond the outlines of black trees. I start walking again. The trail meanders through thick woods, rising and dropping, its bed clogged with roots and large stones that crop up unexpectedly. When I fiddle with the flashlight, surprisingly, it comes on, but its light seems alien now. In a world of ghostly brush and trees, I blink at clumps of dry whitish grass or the faint, swordlike shapes of ferns. Crickets dimple the dark with their calling.

From now on the light works intermittently, but even without it I can make out boulders or logs sprawled in the path. Near the trail, oceans of ceanothus give off a faint glow. Under black trees, mist still skeins the river. Weeds have soaked me to the knees with dew. When the trees break away, I can see the river clearly, a pale band of foam notched here and there by boulders. The light kindles me, and as if to assist its rising, I pick up my pace.

On the bank, a riprap of granite, roots, and moss bears a dark watermark. Current is an image of "horizontal" time, but its depth and fluctuation, like the layered bank, give time a vertical dimension we can wade or dive into. Where a creek spills from a high ledge, I wade through chest-deep sedge to fill my water bottle

and, turning, find myself eye to eye with a large green locust
gnawing on a blade of grass. It's about six inches long, bigger than
any hopper I've seen, an elegant chewing-machine with wings,
avatar of Buddha feasting on green until it *is* green.

Tat twam asi.

That art thou.

When I began my hike in the dark, I neglected to leave behind
my watch. Seeing it now reminds me of my fitfulness and haste.
When I slip it off, the oval of exposed skin shines like a beacon of
my ignorance. The natural world is a living spatio-temporal
continuum, or network, of living time. As urbanites we "time"
ourselves in numerous mechanical ways—with digital watches,
commuter schedules, appointments (the word is telling) and a
linear sense of life's routine progression.

On the river, the notion that time flows becomes more than a
convenient metaphor. Time is no abstraction, but the pulse
of the moving world—sap flowing in the trees, sugars in the veins
of the leaves, or small creeks trickling down the canyon walls to
join the larger flow, which meanders in calm deep stretches,
then drops over waterfall or foams and thunders through rapids.
And there are other imperceptible, manifold flowings. I walk in
waves of invisible light. In my veins blood runs, pulsing. Even
the stones I pass, those at least that are igneous, show signs of the
liquid stage in geologic time. What the river wears smooth will
turn eventually to sand and flow toward the timeless sea.

In the few hours left me, I move to different measures. Light through
the conifers deepens the green of thimbleberry and ninebark.
Where trees tower above me, the day ripens to a green that's deeper
still. By midmorning I've caught and released many cutthroat, but
I'm saddened to have inadvertently taken one life. From a high
ledge, I hooked the fish, but I couldn't get down to the water
quickly enough to free it. I watched it belly-drift downstream, food
for otter, eagle, or some alert raccoon.

The incident reminds me of the distinction between *thou* and *it*. I want to treat the river as a "thou," the way I feel "it" treats me. I want to bring back into daylight the mysterious connection I felt with the river at night; to show the river ever greater respect, not merely use it for the instrumental act of fishing.

I have argued with friends about the ethics of catch-and-release fishing, and of sportfishing in general. I agree that a hooked fish suffers trauma. Imagine: Your mouth has been pierced by a steel hook that tears into your flesh. The line connected to the hook drags you mouth-first out of the river, and, for a minute or longer, you're out of your element, unable even to breathe. You shudder and flail, desperate to escape and reenter the world that sustains you.

But this way of thinking may obscure something that runs deeper. Suffering, per se, may not be the issue here. True, one life comes at the expense of another's. In stressing a cutthroat, I am guilty as charged. But by fishing, I am also privileged with a first-hand, "live" engaging of the wild, a part of it that's elusive and would otherwise remain unseen. When I catch and release a trout, I don't experience the fish as an object, an "it," but as a beautiful slippery life, quivering from the river into my hands. If in being caught the fish nourishes me, as food for body or spirit, are the trauma and suffering I have inflicted on it worthwhile? Can the pain I have given be viewed as a sacrifice, allowing me a renewal and a connection to the rhythms of the natural world? In mythological terms, the god of the river has given itself. The awareness of causing pain should heighten the fisherman's sense of responsibility and respect. And practically speaking, healthy trout populations in catch-and-release rivers suggest the pain may be bearable.

Catching wild trout is a rare privilege. Hooking a fish quickly and releasing it while it's still in the water minimizes injury. I do not seek to inflict harm, but to receive, however briefly, a gift of connecting with what is primal and sustaining. I feel something akin to what Paleolithic hunters must have experienced—a respect for life and the sorrow for having to harm or take it. My accidental killing bears the fruit of a perennial lesson: I must fish with greater respect and never forget the extent of my power to destroy.

At midday I nod off against a middle-aged pine. When I wake, a bright green beetle has landed on my wrist. Perhaps it has mistaken me for some exotic plant. Dreaming, waking, we inhabit parallel worlds. The beetle is a brilliant emerald, like a ringstone with legs and wings. Its feelers sway like metronomes, and when I stretch and yawn, it flies off, a speck in the blaze of noon.

A kingfisher passes on its way upriver. It will not only catch fish, but eat them. In countless ways we are part of each other. Coming and going, we make the rounds of our respective journeys, part of an ever larger, ever more intricate world.

☞ ☞ ☞

When I look up from the campstove, my daughter is kneeling by the river. Earlier, she had picked wildflowers and arranged them in a Folger's can on the camp table. They aren't so much flowers as the weeds of late summer—yarrow and chicory; a withered umbel of cow parsnip; a few asters somehow still blooming. She has changed her mind about keeping them. One by one she tosses the blossoms to drift downstream. As they float away, late sun catches the fringes of her hair. In a flash of absolute clarity I know this moment will remain forever emblazoned in my mind. In another month she will be thirteen. What is most dear is fully present, yet passes away before my very eyes.

☞ ☞ ☞

There's a tingling on my right shin. An ant has humped over sere grass to crawl up my pantleg. Over the river a western tanager flashes into a cedar and lands. Though I'm worn out, I want to stay longer, but it's late in the afternoon. I must walk swiftly to get back while it's still light, though the idea of hiking in the dark is not so intimidating now.

I hike back on the same stretch of trail I covered at night, but nothing looks familiar. The solitude that at night seemed chill and oppressive now bears the weight of my weariness, and it's a good way to be tired. I pass a pool of water so clear I could sit down in the living room of trout and ouzel. Stones on the bottom glow deep olive and appear magnified, as if the river were staring back.

I pass ceanothus and scrub oak singed by frost, the leaves ocher and burnt gold. Clumps of grass look bleached and wheaten, dew no longer enough to sustain it. Rounding a bend, I meet a lone backpacker resting on a log. He has taken a sip from his water bottle and glances up half-startled at my approach. He is bearded, younger than I, sweat glistening on his forehead. We nod at each other, but neither of us speaks. Civilized pleasantries are unnecessary here. The wilderness is a bond of respect we share.

I reach the trailhead near dark. The day is now a completed cycle, a round in the wheel of time. An owl flies across the river and vanishes into the trees. Each life is an enigma, pained and alone, yet also beautiful, part of the whole. The owl embodies a knowledge millennia old. In each cell of its body runs the current of a living code, a tapestry woven of genes and features of landscape it carries as instinct (literally "pricked" or "touched"), an unselfconscious in-dwelling our own species so often seems bent on destroying. Seeing the owl makes me keenly aware of what in this life I sense but can never fully understand. Flesh is like water, bearing what moves from the source, returning to a source still deeper. I slough my pack, walk down to the river, kneel and splash my face. I cup my hands. The water on my lips is cold, traceless.

Hours later, as I approach Lewiston, the moon shines on the Clearwater River. When it catches my hands on the steering wheel, my skin glitters, flecks of troutscale like the river's tiny jewels. In the current, if I look from the corner of my eye, the river seems almost to float the sky. Approaching the city in the spangle of ever-changing beams, I catch a glint that for a second says earth and sky, mind and river, are one.

Winter Crossing

Leslie Leek

The dream:

I'm stunned. The angry mob surges down the narrow street and up to my door. They yell, chant slogans, beat drums and cymbals. They carry billowing cloth banners printed in Chinese characters. It's a scene out of the Cultural Revolution.

"You must leave this apartment," the spokesman says. The others shout "Shame! Shame!" in a language I can't speak.

"There is too much room here for one person," he warns. Then he's caught up with the mob who roil off in a current of voice, drum and cymbal. I stand alone in my spacious apartment. It's old but full of light that plays on primary color: blue walls, red table, green chair. What will I do? I'm frightened, angry, lost.

Bill Studebaker appears. "Come on," he says casually, "I'll help you move your things." He sits in the green chair at the red table. I stand behind him and lean over to give him a kiss on the lips. I'm grateful. I feel safe and happy. The dream ends.

In reality, a few days later I do kiss Bill Studebaker. Although he's the one who leans over the back of my chair in my house in

Pocatello to kiss me good-bye. It's like the dream, I say. Or maybe I just think it. It's like the dream.

I sit at the dining room table with men I love. Steven, my companion, Rick, Harald, and Bill Studebaker. We eat bean soup Steven made and drink red wine and Dickel Number 17. As usual the conversation goes from the somber to the absurd. We laugh until it hurts. Language flies in all directions. The poets volley puns and indulge in flights of fancy that always end in love. We've been to the memorial service for our friend, a poet who shot himself. His father said it was a miracle he lived so long, maybe his wife and daughter kept him, he said. The last time we saw him, he sat in the chair where Bill sits now. He came to see Steven after Steven's heart attack. We shared soup for lunch. He stared out the window into his own conversation. There are endless stories about his life, his writing, manuscripts found piled in old shacks; so many poems mumbled in a sore throat, spit out true but not pretty.

"What a year," we say. "What a goddamn year." Maybe we don't say this out loud; maybe it's a silent phrase that has us all by the throat and turns fear and sorrow into manic jokes about our own deaths. Bill insists he knows everything because he's died the most often and lived to tell about it. What a year: Bill and his wife, Judy, nearly crushed by the accident with the semi, Steven's heart, "a pickax through the back," he says, and five by-passes later he's finally up to mixing broth and beans to comfort everyone. A friend's mother took a last walk in the mountains with vodka and pills, away from the pain. Too many friends have cancer. We don't want to count anymore. We pray, chant, keep candles burning, put pictures of our loved ones on the refrigerator, call their children who keep vigil in hospitals or bedsides, call their names in our sleep.

Bill says, "It's good you dream of us, that keeps us alive."

What a year. My fiftieth year. My winter crossing.

I wedge myself into the hollow of lava rock where my body fits just right. I give myself like the old ones left by their tribes to die. Shoshone, Bannock, other? Not a heartless act but the understanding of survival. Were the old ones grateful to meet their death in contemplation along an old and looping tributary with no worry about their loved ones, just an even trade of breath and winter wind and starry night?

⌐⌐⌐

I dreamed once that I died: I'm a revolutionary. My comrades and I escape on a train in Eastern Europe, Poland, I think. When the train slows, we get off and disguise ourselves with a group of peasants who trudge across a barren brown landscape toward a village. We hide in an abandoned house. The wind surrounds the thin wooden walls with a low moan of loss. We sit in a circle. Our leader says what we know he must, "They're coming. We have no choice." We understand. He pulls out a pistol and shoots each of us in the head. Then he shoots himself. He's just finished when the soldiers come. "Too late," they say. They curse, then leave. I'm dying. I'm slumped against the wall. I see the small neat hole between my eyes. I see the soldiers and even hear their curses. I see my compatriots, all dead. But I feel peaceful. Life ebbs away in slow and lazy loops and curls. I'm overwhelmed with relaxation. This is true contentment. I'm gone.

Was it like that for the old people? I like to think so. One last ritual in the rocks to honor the earth with.

I'm here to consider my own winter crossing. I've turned fifty. Poetry, legend, dreams, love, sorrow, fiction bring me to this place where Marsh Valley stretches along the Bannock range in cold stillness. Marsh Creek, doddering old water flow, winds a course through sacred territory to give itself to Portneuf and Snake. These are creases in the old face of the state shadowed by high desert and volcanic rock that create a plain that surges full of wind and longing through mountains of Idaho.

My back against strong rock, I want to remember the most recent dream that brought me here. New Year's Eve, the dream: I step into a sleek dark gondola for the crossing. Charon's at the helm. I'm surprised to realize he's a man I love but no longer see. Quietly he rows me through the dark and dangerous water. Wraiths of mist rise and coil around us. That's all I remember. It's enough. I can't shake the image: a man I love rows me across Styx? Is it Lethe? I don't remember reaching the other side or what happens there. I don't even know which side is which. Is waking the other side, and I'm on it, and don't realize it?

This man, Charon, or the man who took his place, saved me once. One summer he drove me through the hills around Fort Hall in his pickup truck. We hiked to the top of Mt. Putnam, drank wine and beer, laughed like crazy in the dusk heavy with the smell of sage and juniper. He saved me from the island of my anxiety. One day he took me to a sacred place. This wasn't a dream. "It's the woman's place," he said. "You need to be here. Come on."

We walk up the creek, a wild little tributary. I think he misleads me about its name. I know I belong here although we've already had two encounters with tribal police who warn us I should have a permit to be on the premises. I understand the reasons: my eyes so blue and name so upright and hard. We get to a place where the water tumbles over a fall of amber rocks and splashes into a pool, clear jade or zircon in color. All my life my energy has headed this direction, but how did he know? "Go ahead," he says, "get in. I'll go down the creek a ways. Keep guard."

I'm timid at first. I take off my shoes and socks, put my feet in the water. It's cold. He looks from his place downstream. "Go on," he says.

I take the rest of my clothes off. The breeze feels good. I need a force of will to get in. Finally I sit in the water, then pull myself under. The cold is a shock. I surface and whoop from cold and ecstasy. When my body gives up its boundaries, I relax and say a prayer of thanks for my life, this water, all things. When I get out of the pool I cry. I can't stop. All my fear and sorrow has surfaced.

I sob and keen and shudder. My friend comes back. He holds me. He says, "Here, lie close to the earth. You'll come back to yourself."

My father used to tease me, say that he and Mother found me under a sagebrush on the Snake River Plain, not far from this place. I felt this to be a great compliment, a sign of my belonging in the western landscape. After some time in the dirt, grass, and sunshine, I returned to familiar territory in one piece. But that was too many years ago, before menopause and the thin edge of panic about time running off without me. Good rituals must be renewed. They don't hold forever.

If I could choose a way to cross any wild river, Styx, Lethe, Snake, it would not be by boat. It would be on the back of my strong red mare, Copper Lady. She would take me safely across, swimming if she had to. I'd go with my father giving me a hand up to the stirrup. He'd say, "Your hair shines in the light just like the mare's—two sorrels." Though mine is a trick of light, brown with a few good moments. Now gray. My senses still hold the exhilaration of running the barrels on Copper Lady, our hearts, our muscles working as one. She was a quarter horse–thoroughbred mix made for power and speed. Someone once said, "She's too much horse for such a little gal."

I'm a Sagittarian. My dreams are full of horses and horses in my family have discovered life and death not far from these rocks. My father said, "When I die I'll get on my old black gelding and we'll lift to the sky." I'd follow if I could, my own mare waiting.

I see how we hold the great stories of our lives in language that forms a pattern to shape us. When we repeat them, even to ourselves, we do it word for word as if passing prayer to our children before sleep. Each word an entrance to the nether life. I've hung my parents' death stories on such a pattern. I repeat them often to myself, always with the same rhythm and breath, stories engraved by the senses. It's not my place to tell them here, but to reveal their form in space.

My father's story always starts like this: Fifteen below zero. My
sister and I stay at the house in Dubois. For three days after
Christmas our father releases his hold on life. Sometimes he can
sit at the kitchen table with a cup of coffee in front of him,
though he's far from able to drink. His hands make a rhythmic
movement. We realize he's feeding the newspapers into the Lee
Press for the *Clark County Enterprise* or the *Bannock County News*.
He's riding his craft of fifty years. The last night he no longer sits
or kneels from pain by his chair close to the oil stove counting
"little oriental soldiers" who, he says, wage wars on the carpet.

Fifteen below zero. I put *The Best of Pavarotti* on the stereo because
our father loves Caruso, but Pavoratti is as close as we can get.
We spend the evening with him in the bedroom. We whisper.
We chant:

> We love you, Daddy.
> You're safe.
> You're home in the house in Dubois.
> We love you.
> It's cold outside. It's not snowing.
> We're here. We love you.

Fifteen below zero. I can't take it. I go for a walk outside. I walk
the streets of Dubois at midnight. Snow on the ground moans
under my step: sky clear, stars sharp blue pain. I walk until I'm
numb, the feeling I've been waiting for. Later, much later, I sit in
my father's big chair. I pull a comforter over my head. I say:

> You're safe.
> We're here.
> You're safe.
> All is well.

I want a prayer to keep fear from entering the house. It's all I can
do. Maybe four o'clock in the morning he says to Nancy, "Well,
I gotta go." We kiss him and whisper our love. We hear the
rattle of breath. We're calm, though our hearts are irrevocably

broken. Nancy cuts his blood-stained T shirt, we remove his bloody underwear, final signs of cancer that consumed him. We bathe and prepare him as women have always done for their loved ones.

Our words were the same when Mother died:

> We love you, Mother.
> You're safe.
> We're here. We love you.

Nancy and I held her. There was no weight in our arms. We were in a strange house where she'd been cared for. This was the final disappearance of a fading woman who left us years ago, lost to Alzheimer's. We were desperate for her to recognize our voices. "Please let us comfort you. Mother. Mother," we said. Her death was sweet and peaceful. She slipped away. We still try to find her.

Not long ago I walked down the hall after teaching a class at Idaho State University and a familiar-looking woman came up to me and said, "Aren't you Leslie Leek?"

"Yes," I replied. "We know each other, don't we?"

"We were in high school together," she said. We talked a bit and as she left she said, "I can't believe you're here, in Pocatello. I always thought you'd do something with your life."

I have only three accomplishments: I was at my father's death, my mother's death, and my son's birth.

I'd like to invent a straightforward story—a fiction based on Janne Goldbeck's poem, "Crossing the Winter River." I'd call it "Winter Crossing." I want it to be a story about a woman who saves her mother. She crosses Marsh Creek, no not dangerous enough, the Portneuf? No, the Snake, the Snake River. A story so heroic it's the heart of family legend. It would start like this:

〜〜〜

It's fifteen below, Charlotte leads the strong sorrel mare from the
barn. She's wrapped in a wool coat of her husband's and a hat
that belongs to her son. No matter what her husband and
mother-in-law say about the danger of crossing the river and
the meanness of the cold, she has a premonition her mother is in
danger. The feeling explodes in her. She must get to her
quickly.

"What about the river?" Avery, her husband, asks. "How will you
get across?"

"We'll walk over the ice. If it's not frozen, we'll ford it."

"But it's too cold. You'll freeze to death."

"We'll make it. We have to."

"No. I forbid you to do this."

"Fine," she says and pulls herself up on the mare and they leap off
toward the river.

Charlotte and the mare come to the crossing, She can't read the ice
under the snow. There's no telling where it's rotten, no discerning
the weak places. "Let's go," she says to the mare. "Let's think of the
winged horse." They walk straight across as one breath, one heart.
They take it slow and steady. The ice moans, cracks, "rays and webs,"
as Janne Goldbeck describes it in her poem. They make it, but
have no time to celebrate the crossing because it's still a mile to
the house set apart in some cottonwood trees. Charlotte can tell
something's wrong. Then she sees her mother at the bottom of the
porch steps. Charlotte dismounts before the mare can stop. She
reaches her mother who says in a wisp of a voice, "Charlotte dear,
is that you? I knew you'd come. I seem to have slipped on the stairs."
Charlotte carries her mother into the house. She gets the doctor
and puts the mare in her mother's barn out of the cold. She puts

her arms around the mare's sorrel neck, kisses the strong jaw. "Thank you," she whispers. Her mother has a broken leg, some banged-up ribs, but she'll be all right. She would have frozen to death if Charlotte hadn't crossed the river for her.

Yes, this is a satisfying story—the mother saved.

Over one hundred years later, a father stops his car at a scenic overlook above the great Snake River. He says to his young daughter, "Look there. See the place where the river bends? One terrible winter day when the wind howled and the snow blew so hard you could hardly see the barn from the house, your great-grandmother Charlotte rode her sorrel mare across the dangerous ice in that spot. There was no stopping her. Somehow she knew her mother, your great-great-grandmother would die if she didn't get to her. Charlotte risked everything. That's the kind of blood you have, my sweet. Nothing can stop you."

⌒⌒⌒

The girl's heart and mind are on fire. She wants to write a story. She's burning to put the words in her blue notebook, a story about a woman crossing the ice on her brave sorrel mare to save her mother. The story will start, "It was fifteen below zero."

⌒⌒⌒

Emmylou Harris sings a Leonard Cohen song I almost can't listen to because it creates a mysterious pathway to my heart, a prayer for the cowgirl whose horse ran away.

⌒⌒⌒

I come back to my shape in hollow rock. Back from disintegration, the song still in my head. Oh my dears, the places I've been, the places I'm going, searching for language to shape stories, describe sacred place, portray silence, reveal love. Always crossing or dreaming so.

In the end, will I give up the need to shape dream and articulation? Will I open my hand and mouth to let breath assume any shape it wants as it swells into the currents of Styx, Lethe, Marsh Creek, Portneuf, Snake?

⌒⌒⌒

I'm brought back to myself in the rock by the sigh, swallow and gulp of old Marsh Creek. These sounds remind me that when I stay at the cabin on the Salmon River I hear the voices of women on the river at night. I listen as if my life depended on it, ghost voices. I think they belong to Judy, Rose, Margaret, my sister Nancy, and others I love. I imagine how they dance, cavort, gossip, tell tales and reveal dreams around a fire on a sandbar. I want to be there.

⌒⌒⌒

Now I too sigh, swallow, gulp air full of sage, rock crevice, slow water on its way to Portneuf, Snake, a convergence in Hells Canyon. Why am I honored by this Giveaway? Around me the gifts pile up, charms for any crossing: Harald knocks on the door some summer nights to say, "Come outside, look at the moon." Rick gives me the perfect binder for my stories, the one I've been looking for. I watch Brin, my son, grow into a beautiful man. Somewhere Gino Sky leads his illusive character, Jonquil Rose, in a tango of sweet talk across the Snake River Plain. Margaret puts her head close to mine as we whisper our lives. I know exactly how my lips feel against Rose's cheek and the smell of her copper hair. She instructs me in the art of drifting through Fridays with a friend. Margaret and I learn well. Judy puts her arms around me, rubs my neck. I can always find my way by the sound of her laughter and the strength of her heart. Nancy gives me everything.

I hear Margaret's voice, "Les, I love you." The words undulate across the creek, over the rock, through the evening air like my father's whistle when he called the horses in this very place, when he called me in from play. It's time to go home.

My heart beats into the breath of evening. I've been here so long
I'm not sure I can move. The point is, I can move. I stand up with
difficulty. I'm starving. When I left home this morning Steven was
making a thick tomato sauce. It's been simmering all day and
there'll be spaghetti and crusty bread and red wine. He'll be
wearing the apron printed with grapes I gave him for his birthday.
He'll have music cranked up loud: Springsteen, Pavarotti. The cat
will be asleep on the back of the couch.

The horse lights he gave me will glow sweetly in greeting as they
arch between the living room and dining room, a string of leaping
ponies to show the way.

Real River

Lesa Luders

The only obstacle the salmon have not been able to overcome was the
pouring of concrete across their rivers.

—Cecil Andrus, past governor of Idaho

I teach at the university in Moscow, Idaho, a small college town,
in the midst of wheat, pea, and lentil fields, where the plaid of
brown fallow intermixes with bright green. My partner and I live
in a cabin, and outside are wheat fields. Last summer I found an
arrowhead in the overturned ground. Before there were any white
people in Idaho, the Nez Perce Indians hunted in *Tat-kin-mah,*
"the place of the little spotted deer." I have an early edition of
Hear Me, My Chiefs!, containing Nez Perce legend and history,
given to me by my father. It has traveled with me as I moved from
place to place and finally settled here.

The nearest river to me is the Snake. In 1833, Captain Benjamin
L.E. Bonneville traveled down the Snake River, and Washington
Irving published an account of his exploration:

> At times, the river was overhung by dark and stupendous
> rocks, rising like gigantic walls and battlements; these
> would be rent by wide and yawning chasms, that seemed

to speak of past convulsions of nature. Sometimes the river was of a glassy smoothness and placidity, at other times it roared along in impetuous rapids and foaming cascades. Here, the rocks were piled in the most fantastic crags and precipices; and in another place they were succeeded by delightful valleys carpeted with greensward. The whole of this wild and varied scenery was dominated by immense mountains rearing their distant peaks into the clouds.

The Snake River used to be rich in salmon, until the four hydroelectric dams on the lower Snake began mixing power and blending up the salmon in their turbines. From 1990 to 1998, only sixteen sockeye salmon made it back to their ancestral home. One salmon returned in 1998. *One.* Helen Chenoweth, member of Congress from Idaho, said, "How can I [take the salmon's endangered-species status seriously] when you can buy a can in Albertson's?" In protest, bumper stickers appeared on cars: *Can Helen, Not Salmon.* I carry that sticker on my car.

⌒⌒⌒

By heredity, I am an environmentalist, passed to me by my father, a schoolteacher. In the summers my parents built a cabin in the mountains, near the rugged Canadian border, three hours north of our hometown of Spokane, Washington. My father was a burly man who could lift a tree. As he piled wood, he would say, "It goes there, Sis." Soon the woodpile would be at his chest, his neck, and when it was even with his eyes, he would be done. He taught me to pile wood and so much more. Perhaps he also taught me how to tell a story, placing each word with a certain integrity.

Spokane is less than two hours' drive from Moscow, and I visit my parents monthly. Dad has always been a teller of stories—true, fact-based stories. He is extremely reserved, but he becomes animated when he tells a story. From him, I learned about northwestern fur trappers, Abraham Lincoln, Apollo Thirteen, the American Revolution, World War II, Lewis and Clark, the Cold

War, and the variety of trees that grow in the Northwest. I learned a great deal of information, but I never learned how to have an actual conversation with him.

He talks like this: "Before 1871, there was no Germany. Then all of the German principalities were unified into one force, and out of that came modern Germany. Our family came from the principality of Pomerania, which is on the Slavic end of Germany. My grandfather was a sergeant major. He was a big man for those days because the average height was 5'6". He was 6'2". After he had secreted his parents on board ship, he murdered his commanding officer and fled Germany. He met his wife in America."

When I was a child and first heard the story, I nourished it and changed the facts: my great-grandfather was sick to death of his commanding officer, who was always making moves on my great-grandfather's wife, so he had a duel with him and won, put his wife on a boat, and fled the country. In the United States he worked in the barren fields, had insomnia, and spoke passionately about his dreams.

"Of course, our last name is German. *Luders*. It means *rotten wretch*." My father rubbed his chin. "No wonder they left Germany."

I looked the word up in a German dictionary. *Luders* was defined as *pinhead, bitch,* and *luck*.

Pinhead? That meaning underwent a revision: I was a Lucky Bitch—glad to be one, thank you—with pinhead deleted.

⌐⌐⌐

I was on one of my monthly visits to see my parents last summer. My father had moved outside in his lawn chair while my mother sprayed her petunias. It was midafternoon, and the heat of August was very strong. My mother, with her head of pure white hair, had perspiration on her upper lip, and my bald-headed father had beads of sweat trailing down his brow.

"I wish this heat would break," Mom said.

Something about the rushing of the hose must have made my father think about a canoe trip he took down the Snake River years ago. He pulled his chair beneath the awning to avoid the light of the sun.

"There are roughly ninety-three thousand miles of rivers and streams in the state of Idaho. Did you know that?"

I smiled. "How do you remember all that information?"

"My mind is a bear trap. Nothing escapes. I probably told you about the trip we took down the Snake River?"

"I'd like to hear it again, though. I love that story." I knew it by heart, and images of the Snake appeared before he spoke again.

"Sis, a gossamer substance formed on the weeds, light and filmy. Out on the river the waves were undulant. It was beautiful."

I gained my vocabulary from him. When I was eight years old, I won a spelling bee: antidisciplinarianism. From my mother, I learned down-home common sense. She speaks like she was raised on the hips of Texas, but she has never been there.

"When did you travel the Snake River? Was it in the fifties?"

"Back in the early sixties, before the countryside was flooded by dams, we canoed down the Snake—when the Snake was a real river. Did you know that the Snake is a major tributary of the Columbia River? Every second, it pours 50,000 cubic feet of water into the Columbia.

He took that trip with Ev. Ev and Dad had been friends since they wore raggy shoes to grade school in the Great Depression. My father always refers to Ev with three names: Poor Old Ev.

"Poor Old Ev and I, and of course my Labrador, Jill, put the canoe in at Lewiston. Jill had earned that trip. She had hunted her heart out all over that territory. Pheasant, ducks, chukar, quail. From Lewiston to Penawawa, there were flocks of 150 quail. Orchards sided the Snake. Apricots, peaches—the climate was so good they could grow soft fruit. We used to go down there when you were a kid."

"I don't remember."

"You were just a little kid, then."

He was wearing shorts and so was I, but Mom wore cotton-polyester pants. The heat was rising up to ninety and above.

"We went the end of July. If you think this is hot, try canoeing down the Snake River. We brought enough water to last through the trip, but didn't expect it to reach 110 degrees. Record temperatures. Our water lasted two days. We went into the old homesites. The Corps of Engineers had condemned all the ranches on the riparian area of the river. The farmers were ordered out, their ranches foreclosed. For a while they leased them out to get some profit, because it took years for the Corps to build the dam. But eventually all the ranches were flooded. From Lewiston to Wawawai, Riperia, and Penawawa."

"We got water from the wells of the homesites. It had a high alkali content and didn't set well with us. It gave us diarrhea. We're paddling and perspiring and the sun is beating down on us, and we have the G.I.s."

My mother sprayed water onto her petunias. "In five days, Edward lost twenty pounds to dehydration."

"They raised apricots down there. Beautiful farmland, lot of hay. Riley Ranch, which is just above the bridge, used to raise rodeo stock. I knew old man Riley, a nice old rugged pioneer. But now the riparian zone of the lower Snake River is gone. Everything's gone. Railroads, homesteads, orchards, towns—all of it underwater. All the native grass and brushes were flooded, which had a dramatic impact on wildlife. The islands in the river, which were breeding places for many birds, were destroyed. Colonies of terns, cormorants, and ring-billed gulls were wiped out.

"They also destroyed the fishery. Steelhead, salmon—they're still trying to play games with those fish. Those dams on the lower Snake River account for the majority of juvenile fish kills. The fish must run the rivers, and the rivers are blocked with dams. Tinkering with inadequate flow volumes doesn't save the fish. If you ask me, the dams should be removed, and the Snake River should be drawn down."

My mother teased, "Why don't you run for governor?"

He ignored her. "So anyway, we entered the Snake River at Lewiston and went downstream. We had a seventeen-foot canoe and six hundred pounds of gear—sleeping bags, Dutch oven, two ice chests, water, and food. The first two days, before the ice melted in the ice chest, we had bull neck for dinner—"

This was the first time he had talked about the food. "Bullnick?"

My mother laughed. "Cattle, silly. They use it to make hamburger."

"Bull neck." He gripped his neck. "It was imported from Australia. The rest of our stuff was freeze dried. By the end of the first day, half of all the drinking water was gone. We had a six-pack of beer that we dragged along behind the canoe, we thought the water would cool it, but by the time we camped the beer was tepid, the water was that hot. We drank the warm beer the first night out."

But all those homesteads sat there dormant in anticipation of the floodwaters. We had camped downstream at a sandbar where there had been a homestead, and we were cooking our meat. A truck came down, and a man, maybe in his mid-fifties, said to us, 'What are you doing?'

"'We're canoeing down the Snake, while it's still a real river.'

"He said, 'This was my granddad's homestead. I've lived here all my life. Two years ago they told me I'd have to leave. You can tell by looking at me and my rig that we were never prosperous, but this place had a lot of sentimental value. We raised hogs and chickens, cattle for beef and milk, we had a small orchard, and a hell of a lot of blackberries. I don't know what I'm going to do, don't know.'"

My father massaged the top of his bald head. "Poor old guy, I hope he made it."

"He did," Mom said.

"How do you know he made it? You weren't even there."

"And how do you know he didn't?"

He stared at the bird feeder he had built in his yard. It was crowded with chirping flickers, goldfinches, and juncos. "We went on down the Snake and saw archaeological digs with crews from the University of Idaho and Washington State University. We ran into a group of college students digging at very shallow caves called *rockshelters*. We saw the Marmes Rockshelter which held remnants of prehistoric humans. Sis, the bones of Marmes Man are among the oldest documented remains ever found in the Western Hemisphere, carbon-dated to be ten thousand years old. I was able to see the old bones covered by a canvas. I took some pictures of it but they don't show much. The site was flooded by waters of the Lower Monumental Reservoir.

"If you look at all the archaeological sites, they represent isolated bands of hunters and gatherers. Aboriginal man ate from his surroundings—elk, deer, and pronghorn antelope. Bison, fish, birds, bighorn sheep. Endemic groups of the Columbia basin were populated all along the Lower Snake River. Look at man's ancestors—they are there."

☙☙☙

Look at my ancestors: both of them, there before me. My mother and my father. Recently, the doctors had told my father that he had colon cancer. Chemotherapy was an option, but he chose not to do it. He would undergo surgery instead. When I got a phone call, both of them spoke on separate telephones. Mom—who doesn't cry—began to sob.

"We'll wait and see," she said. "But I can't bear to talk about it."

He told me about the cancer, speaking in a stilted voice: "We're just going to take this a week at a time.... But, you know, Sis, I am in control of my own destiny. Me alone."

There was no fiction this time. No make-believe. No fantasy. The truth.

I spit out, "I'm sorry, Dad."

He was silent.

My mom replied, "We're taking it a day at a time."

"I'll let you go now," Dad said. His line went dead.

"Mom?"

"I'm here."

"Could you tell him that I love him?"

"Dad," she called to him. "Lesa wants to say something to you."

"Hello again, Sis."

"I want you to know that I love you."

In his voice I heard a smile. "This isn't even Father's Day."

"I wanted you to know."

"Well, of course I knew that, but thank you for telling me."

⌒⌒⌒

My mother watered her tomato bush. "Tell her about the three girls." She sprayed water near his feet.

"What girls?" Dad teased.

"*The* girls."

He chuckled. "We came around a bend, it was hot, about one o'clock in the afternoon, and there were three girls out sunbathing in the nude. We paddled over just as fast as our little paddles would go. The girls weren't embarrassed, but they did stroll back and put on some clothes."

"Well I hope so," Mom said.

"There was a graduate student in charge of that particular dig. He had seven students under him. They did a good job, but lived a rather free lifestyle. And in the sixties that wasn't so uncommon.

"He asked us, 'What are you doing?'

"'Canoeing down the Snake, while it's still a real river.'

"He said, 'That's something I'd really like to do.'

"Poor Old Ev answered, 'Why don't we switch places?'

"That gave me the giggles. When I was younger, I used to get the giggles quite a little bit. Really get the giggles. Seriously get the giggles. I was kept out of places because I got the giggles."

"Really?" I had never seen this big burly man curled over in giggles.

"So anyway, Poor Old Ev and I had some good times and some bad times on that trip down the Snake River. Paddling, perspiring, and

G.I.s. The last night we pulled the canoe up, and we were completely
dehydrated and exhausted. We had brought along some
parachute material and put it up as mosquito netting and then
collapsed. The next morning the canoe was gone, because
the water level had been raised. It was a quarter of a mile out,
stuck on an island. We flipped. Poor Old Ev had to swim out to
get it.

"That day we were hoping to get out of the slackwater. Whenever
there's a rapid, there's a breeze. Sis, it's like taking a cold shower.
But we went through rapids and were caught in a pool, and our
seventeen-foot aluminum canoe started to bend in the middle. I
was in front, Poor Old Ev in back. We paddled like hell until we
were free. It felt like we were attached to a slingshot. We moved
out of the vortex, so that the rapids would shoot us out.

"That was the most dangerous part of the trip, being caught in the
rapids with a crooked canoe. The sun and the heat were so bad,
we were sunburned under our chin, nose, and ears. We would
jump in the river and it was like jumping into a bathtub. We'd get
out and steam would rise off our bodies.

"The last thirty miles there was no current. That means there was
no breeze—a gigantic, unmerciful furnace. We became numb.
Paddle. Paddle. Paddle. Stroke. Stroke. Stroke. The Snake, with all
its winds and bends was about 140 miles. It took us five nights and
six days. I don't think we could have made another."

My mother left the hose spraying in the yard and stood behind
him with her hands on his shoulders. "Good thing you didn't. Your
wife was waiting."

"I told you I'd be home in six days."

I put my hand on his knee. "Tell me about when you and Mom met."

"You don't know that?" he asked. "I was twenty. She was twenty-
one—an older woman."

"That's me." Mom pulled out a lawn chair and sat down. "From Spirit Lake, Idaho, meeting this handsome young man from the big city of Spokane."

"I asked Winnifred out on a date and she agreed. We were married. Then we had you kids. That's about it, Sis."

"Didn't you get in a fight at your wedding reception?"

"Sure. In my younger days I had a lot of drinking buddies. I didn't invite them to the wedding, but they came anyway, and they were going to steal Mom. When they set their hands on your mom, I got mad and started swinging. Your uncles—Mom's brothers— came to help. It was a dramatic way to get married. Very dramatic."

"They wanted us to be apart on our wedding night." Standing behind him, Mom wrapped her arms around him. "It took me awhile to get used to his name. I kept signing our checks with my maiden name."

"Winnifred Olin," he said.

"Winnifred Luders."

"Luders," I said. "It means luck, did you know?"

"Luders, in German, means luck?"

"That's one of its meanings."

He stared at a goldfinch flying away. Suddenly he turned to me. With his index finger, he pointed to his skull. "All of this—all the information, all the data, all the facts—will vanish with me. All of this will be gone."

I looked into his cloudy blue eyes. "I'll remember them, Dad."

His gaze shifted to the sky. "Luders means luck, you say?"

"That's right."

"So if I'm out fishing and getting skunked, I'll want some luck…that's the time I'll ask for my own name—Luders—which stands for luck?"

"Yes."

"And when I'm heading to surgery, that's the time I'll want some luck, some Luders?"

He looked at a red-winged blackbird that had come to feed. "But those salmon. Sis. They hovered in the river, their mouths opening and closing. Their spotted backs were splotched with white from the journey. Their fins were frayed. But they made it home. To spawn and die."

"Dad?" I knew the answer, but asked the question anyway. "What color were the salmon?"

"Red."

"Fiery red, like the sun rising?"

"A surge of life." He smiled as he watched the red-winged blackbird nip at a sunflower seed. "The indomitable energy of life itself."

My father remembered the man who had lost his homestead to the waters of the dam, who had waited for the Snake to rise, destroying his orchard, his stock, his blackberries, his homestead, his life.

My father remembered.

That memory was mine.

To spawn is to die is to live, if one person remembers.

Angling the St. Maries

Ron McFarland

I was born on the banks of the mighty Ohio River, in Bellaire, Ohio, when that city was a blue-collar, working-man's town of steel mills and glass factories, most of which are now rusted phantoms of the power they once represented. My father can remember when the Ohio was so polluted with combustible industrial waste that it periodically caught on fire here and there. For those who care about poetry, that's James Wright country: "We knew even then the Ohio River was dying."

But I grew up during the placid 1950s in Cocoa, Florida, where I roamed happily between two river systems, the Indian River (technically a saltwater lagoon, rank from the stench of oyster beds), which flowed just a mile east of my house, and the St. Johns, with its tepid dark water and lunker largemouth bass that sprawled loosely in channels and lakes about two miles to the west. From its source in Brevard County about thirty miles south of Cocoa, the St. Johns flows northward, emptying into the Atlantic at Jacksonville. At about 285 miles, though, it is a mere rivulet compared to the Ohio, which muscles its way over some 980 miles into that quintessentially American river, the Mississippi.

All my life I have believed there is no such thing as a bad river: there are only good ones and better ones. But I have never lost a

farm or a home to a river, as did some friends who live in Grand
Forks, North Dakota. I try not to be naive in my passion for
flowing water. We who write poems are suspicious enough as it is,
obsessed as we are with language, but I confess to being
obsessed with flowing streams, as well. A drainage ditch behind
my house in Broadmoor Acres, a "housing project" as they were
called in the fifties, was the focal point of my boyhood: a two-
foot-deep, six-foot-wide ecosystem of dragonflies, turtles, frogs,
snakes, and minnows that could measure up to three or four
inches. My favorite fishing device was an old tire casing. So it does
not require the mighty Mississippi to satisfy my craving for
streams, or a custom-built split-bamboo fly rod to indulge my
fishing fantasies.

I came to Idaho in 1970 after three years of angling on the slow,
mud-bottomed streams of central Illinois and western Indiana: the
Embarras (silent "s"), the Sangamon, the Kaskaskia, Sugar Creek,
and the Wabash, where I fought and lost the biggest carp of my
fishing career. Those were the good old days of carp, and black
sucker, and red horse, and freshwater drum—and the retired
English professor who was then my fishing partner insisted we eat
whatever we caught. A flathead catfish or a decent sized bullhead,
or a green or longear sunfish was a real treat. I once had the
misfortune to land a minuscule horned dace. My fishing mentor
recorded it meticulously as he had recorded all the catches in
those streams for some forty years (species, size, time of day, date),
and he demanded that I take it home to the frying pan. The flesh
was firm, white, tasty, and full of little bones.

Those three years on midwestern streams were memorable for
reasons other than what some would contemptuously refer to as
"trash fishing." My fishing pal was Marcus S. Goldman, a
Renaissance scholar and gentleman of the old school. He had
served in the medical corps during World War I and had been
gassed (his senses of taste and smell were still affected by it), and
after the war he had stayed for a while in Paris, where he met the
young Hemingway and others of the Lost Generation—Joyce,
Pound, Ford Madox Ford, Gertrude Stein. He had also served in

the Second World War, and had witnessed nuclear tests at Bikini. We always managed to find something to talk about.

But most of my memories are of the sluggish, murky streams and the draining heat and humidity. This was classic bottom-fishing with bait-casters: stick a worm on a hook with enough lead to keep your line from drifting back to your feet, and wait; tip of the rod twitches; pick it up carefully and pinch the line to feel when the fish takes the worm, then haul it in. It sounds a bit prosaic compared to working lures for bass or casting flies for trout, but at the time it was all I had, and it was enough. I remember one muggy afternoon on Sugar Creek, which was almost the color of butterscotch pudding, that an Amish farmer drove up in his black buggy and we chatted for a good while, but I do not recall what fish I caught that day, if any.

So in the summer of 1970, my wife and newborn daughter and I drove an overloaded Chevrolet van across the country, and the first Idaho river I dipped my hand into was the Lochsa, and that was because a yellow jacket or a deer fly had bitten me. The clear and what then seemed icy cold water flowing over rock excited me beyond expression, and as we followed the Lochsa into the Clearwater, I somehow expected Moscow and the University of Idaho to be around the next bend. They were not. Moscow is located high above the Clearwater, and the treacherous old spiral highway that separates the town from the river made the Clearwater a low priority stream in my book for several years.

The next summer, however, I discovered the St. Maries (pronounced "Mary's," not Marie's") and I have been fishing and romancing that stream ever since, for more than a quarter of a century. And twenty-five years ago you could amble up to that peaceful gurgle of water, and you would almost always be alone, and you could toss in a flesh-colored salmon egg and haul out some respectable native cutthroat along with the planted rainbows, which were so much larger then on the average than they are now that they seemed an altogether different species. Over the years I have lavished my piscatorial affections on just

five or six miles of this little stream, which starts somewhere
between Grandfather and Grandmother Mountain and picks up
trickles from Gramp, Flewsie, and Merry creeks before it reaches
the logging town of Clarkia, where my Uncle Stoney worked one
summer for the Forest Service after he came back from World
War II and the Battle of the Bulge, where he had been wounded,
though not as seriously, it seems, as Hemingway's Nick Adams,
who needed all the mystique the Big Two-Hearted River of upper
Michigan could afford.

Geologists are almost as vague as poets when it comes to rivers.
They will tell us that rivers are "defined" essentially by the fact
that water, under the influence of gravity, flows downhill. But what
is the difference between a creek, brook, stream, rivulet, rill, or
run, and a river? My encyclopedia indicates that in Great Britain
and New England, "streams of all sizes except the smallest
tributaries are called rivers," noting that the Batson River in Maine
is only four miles long. When I visited Lincoln City, Oregon,
about three years ago I remember seeing the D River, which is
claimed to be the world's smallest at about one mile. If I were
making geological policy on the subject, I would insist that in
order to be a river, a stream must have at least one tributary, or
perhaps two. Yes, two or more tributaries should be required of
any self-respecting river. Of course a dictionary will supply a very
sensible hierarchy that runs like this: rill (small brook), brook,
creek (somewhat larger than a brook), river (larger than a creek).
Terms such as "run" and "rivulet" are more vaguely defined as
small brooks, and "stream" is the generic term that covers the
whole confusion. The problem, as any casual traveler or riparian
geologist could tell you, is that many a stream that is firmly
labeled "creek" is longer, deeper, swifter, and broader than many a
stream labeled "river."

The St. Maries is an open, refreshing, welcoming little stream that
hardly rates the designation "river" at all as it flows some forty-
odd miles north to the town of St. Maries, where it meets the
"shadowy St. Joe," a more renowned and spectacular fishing river
by far. But I am a small man of limited ambitions and very limited

talent as an angler. As a student and teacher of seventeenth-century poetry, I am not inclined so much to the epic majesty of Milton as to the lyric gems of Donne, Jonson, Herrick, Traherne, and Marvell. I'm a recreational fisherman, content with a few small trout and not too proud to pass up a stocker. I'm not too proud to tie on a spinner either, if the situation seems to call for it, and I believe the grasshopper and the lowly worm have their seasons. True blue fly-fishers must regard me as a reprobate, or at best only a half-saved sinner.

In *A River Runs Through It*, which I consider to be the ultimate fishing story, Norman Maclean connects inept fly fishing with mankind's fall from grace, and I am sure if he had ever seen me with a fly rod in my hands, he would have found his premise confirmed. Not that I'm much better when I'm casting spinners, lures, or natural baits. Of course there is such a thing as the law of averages, so I have caught a few large fish over the years, including a memorable steelhead on Hammer Creek and an eight-foot-long shark in the Gulf of Mexico, but I prefer the ready-to-hand ease and simplicity of the St. Maries to the complicated fuss-and-bother of the North Fork of the Clearwater, Kelly Creek, the St. Joe, Silver Creek, or Henry's Fork of the Snake, all of which I have fished with modest success at one time or another. Call me lazy. Or maybe it's my fabled impatience that prevents me from investing the time and planning necessary to do justice to the worthier trout venues of Idaho.

But what's not to like about the amiable St. Maries, that companionable slip of a stream? I suppose it's a matter of deciding what you want out of a river. The latter half of the St. Maries, from Fernwood on, is probably floatable or raftable early in the season, but I don't know what you would encounter with respect to rapids—not much, I suspect. I've taken only a couple of rafting trips, and I must confess that my mind kept drifting away from the business at hand to speculate on holes, runs, and riffles. When I saw an osprey swoop off with a large trout while I was drifting down the Snake near Jackson Hole a few years ago, all I could think was that if I had my fly rod with me I'd have jumped ship on the spot.

My obsession with fishing obviously equals that with language and rivers. The St. Maries is an excellent stream beside which to take a stroll or a hike along paths worn by anglers or cattle, but of course, for me, such walking is destined to end in a wet line. When we were first married, my wife actually accompanied me on occasional fishing trips, but that was before she realized that "going fishing" was not, for me, an activity of two or three serene hours, but of six or eight intense hours, whether they're biting or not. The last time she went with me to the St. Maries it was probably to watch our son rather than to admire my inimitable fly-casting style. She spent most of the time in the shade of a small tree, reading a novel.

Of course, one may camp along the St. Maries any number of places where it flows through the St. Joe National Forest, and there is a small, developed campground where the river flows under a bridge on Idaho Highway 2, just a few miles north of Clarkia. You will pass a ranger station just outside of town, where you may acquire further information. Landowners, so far, have been wonderfully tolerant of anglers and other visitors, so I usually make a point of picking up the occasional bit of litter I come across. It's not a big deal, after all, to pick up a piece of packaging from someone's spinner or a stray aluminum can. It's as easy for me to pick up as it is for some careless slob to drop. Maybe I pick it up because it makes me feel superior to the jerk who tossed it aside, so please don't think of me as an altruist. The extent to which I police the area probably has less to do with my concern for others than with my own desire to see the place look its best.

Sometimes I think I'm a man whose eyes are firmly fastened to the ground. I don't look at the sky quite enough, and I fail to regard the stars as I should. But one afternoon as I was splashing across the St. Maries (there are relatively few places in the stretches I fish that would be over even my head), I found a five dollar bill floating at my feet. It was folded neatly in half, and it seemed almost to be swimming on its own. I guess it fell from the pocket of some less fortunate angler, but I recall thinking how remarkable the occasion was, as if it were an omen of some sort, and I wasted little thought on whoever had lost the cash. Retrospectively, I decided whoever had lost the money was probably not as nice a guy as I was anyway. I offer this anecdote as proof that it pays to keep your head out of the clouds and as evidence of my deep disinclination toward altruism. I caught my limit that day, as I often have on the St. Maries (I've been skunked a few times, too, but not very often), so I drove away thinking very highly of myself. Only later did it occur to me that it might just have easily have been a *twenty*.

What is a river *worth?* In the economic scheme of things, I guess the St. Maries is not worth much. You cannot float grain barges on it as you can the Columbia, and you cannot dam it for hydroelectric power and irrigation on a grand scale as you can the Snake, and you cannot even drive a log jam down its length to a sawmill, although small log drives were common to the St. Maries and such tributaries as Emerald Creek until around 1930. Certainly the St. Maries will never be known for its river-cities; it offers no potential New Orleans, St. Louis, Cincinnati, Pittsburgh; not even a Portland, Spokane, or Boise. Nor is it a candidate for "wild and scenic" status. Clarkia boasts a small elementary school and an important site for Miocene fossils (that's 25 million years ago, give or take a decade), from which I have taken specimens of such subtropical species as bald cypress and tupelo, which I associate with rivers like the Suwanee in northern Florida. The area around the Emerald Creek tributary is noted for garnets (the star garnet is the state gem of Idaho, which calls itself "The Gem State" and not, after all, "The Spud State," "Famous Potato" license plates notwithstanding). Fernwood, which was originally Fennwood, boasts a population of more than six hundred, a virtual metropolis relative to Clarkia, eleven miles south, or Santa, two miles north. And after Santa you drive about fifteen miles into St. Maries, population around twenty-five hundred, the seat of Benewah County. Is St. Maries a "thriving" town? I suppose it is, if any town dependent on the timber industry can be safely said to thrive these days.

But by the time you reach St. Maries, you have gone well past the St. Maries River as it flows in my mind's eye. In a way it's a kids' river, a nice river that flows mightiest in the imagination, a fantasy of a river. If I had lived in Clarkia as a boy, it would have been my Old Man River, my Father of Waters. I would have joined my friends at one of several likely swimming holes near town, where occasionally I've seen kids swimming and tubing, and I would have hiked and biked past where Merry Creek puts in, and when I wanted to impress my mother I would have brought home bouquets of camas, buttercups, daisies, cinquefoil, larkspur, Indian paintbrush, fireweed, goldenrod (which would have made my father sneeze)—whatever was available at the time. (As a boy in Florida, my flower of choice was the abundant water hyacinth from the ditch back of our yard, a beautiful purple cluster that wilts with depressing rapidity.) And, of course, I would have fished myself into oblivion.

Not that the St. Maries is a fine trout stream; in fact, it really is not even a "good" trout stream technically, as it cannot sustain a respectable year-around supply of native fish. It is just close to hand, an hour's easy drive from Moscow, and it is familiar, an old friend. I can still pick up occasional native cutthroats on it here and there, but I always return them and hope that the next angler will do likewise. Sometimes I'll hook a good rainbow that I suspect has lasted a couple of summers and not migrated into the St. Joe, as it seems most of the fish do when the river gets low, as it always does in the summer, too low to be fishable really. It certainly is not a good late summer or fall stream, from what I can tell. And I do worry about the impact of cattle along so much of its length, tearing down the banks and adding to the siltation (many stretches of the St. Maries are soft-bottomed and fishless except for suckers), but I've been worrying about that for years.

Rivers have amazing resilience; if not, we'd surely have killed them all by now. My father told me a couple of years ago that the Ohio River looked remarkably cleaner than it had when he was a boy in the 1920s. But I suspect that small streams like the St. Maries are the most vulnerable to human pressures, so I continue to worry. When I am fishing, though, I am not worrying. Early in *A River Runs Through It* Norman Maclean wrote, "One great thing about fly fishing is that after a while nothing exists of the world but thoughts about fly fishing." But later on he had more accurate thoughts on the subject, and he wrote, "It is not fly fishing if you are not looking for answers to questions." The questions he was writing about were both piscatorial and personal, but the point is that when you are fishing, you should not be worrying. In fact, your mind should be so free of the quotidian that you can reflect on important questions and even solve problems, or perhaps dissolve them.

When I am fishing, I do seem to solve a problem from time to time, or answer a question or two, as Maclean proposes, but I guess more often what I find is that the problems and questions simply dissolve. Water, after all, is the universal solvent, if I recall my high school chemistry correctly. As I see it, one virtue of the St. Maries is that, unlike more difficult and challenging streams, it poses few problems of its own; after all, I know where to go if I desire challenge and complexity. It comes down to this for me: When I am fishing, it is what I am *not* thinking about that matters most.

I calculate that two moderately sized paragraphs will accommodate the obligatory fishing story to round out this essay. Yesterday afternoon I drove to the St. Maries near Clarkia and tried my luck: caught a stocked rainbow on an orange roostertail spinner; had no luck with two varieties of flies, an Elk Hair Caddis and a Pale Evening Dun; returned all fish carefully, and apparently none the worse for wear. I then drove a few miles downstream and tied on an Adams with much greater success: six nice cutthroats, all keepers, but reinvested in the stream for possible future withdrawal (I try to keep my accounts in order). The cutthroats will not stay in the St. Maries in any numbers once the water warms up, but a heavy snowpack has kept the stream cool for longer than usual this year. By that time my poor, overworked fly had come unraveled, and my subsequent efforts with a Mosquito and a so-called Parachute Adams came to naught, the latter fly, in fact, being deposited as a permanent feature of a spruce that had fallen across a promising hole. I paused to tie on some fresh 4x tippet, as my leader had shrunk from about four feet to about two. Whenever I tie on fresh tippet instead of changing the leader altogether, I worry that I haven't made a good enough knot or that the knot will weaken the line, but sooner or later it has to be done, and I'm one of those anglers who never has a new leader ready when he needs it.

On the way upstream I had tried a nice run and briefly hooked into what appeared to be a sizable trout, but I could see by the way the water was flowing through that particular hole I was on the wrong side of the stream, so I planned to hit it again on the way back after crossing the river. Where I forded the St. Maries the water reached just high enough to dampen the bottom of my wallet; halfway across I looked to my left and saw that I might have crossed about knee-deep if I'd bothered to study the matter more closely. I'm one of those anglers who cannot stand waders— too costly, uncomfortable and clumsy. Also I'm one of those guys who just doesn't look good in waders. I suspect only tall people look really good in waders.

Okay, make that three paragraphs, but I regard the above as a mere transitional paragraph, hardly worth counting at all. So, by the time I returned to that place where I'd hooked the fish about an hour earlier, I'd gone back to an Adams, but it, too, was looking bedraggled, and the fish, if it was still around, blithely ignored it, so I went back to the old roostertail spinner, fly-fishing apostate that I am. Whap! I locked into a nice cutthroat of the twelve-inch class, and because that stretch of water was producing no stockers, I was sorely tempted to take it home so I would have evidence to show my wife, who tends to be unreasonably incredulous of my angling narratives. But in a gesture of sportsmanship worthy of Papa Hemingway himself, I returned it unharmed, except for a slight puncture in its jaw. Then I recalled having seen a few grasshoppers flicking around back at Clarkia, so I tied on a new Henry's Hopper I had just acquired, and I was pleased with how it rode high in the water and was much easier to see than the little Adams, which was tied on a #12 hook. Whoosh! When a big trout hits, it seems to attack with its entire body. Something about that Hopper must have looked extraordinarily appetizing. It was one of those rare moments in my life as a fisherman that I did *not* try to horse it in, but actually played the fish, let it take some line, keeping the tip up, reeled in, let it take line again, getting anxious when it streamed out of the hole against the far bank and straight across a shallow stretch into another larger hole, reeled in again, worrying about that couple feet of tippet I'd tied on, reeled in, and so on until the fish tired out and came to me. It was a little over sixteen inches long and deep chested, barrel chested by comparison with any trout I had ever taken from the St. Maries. And I did take the fish (when I cleaned her, I found roe), even though she was a cutthroat. I wanted to show her off to my son, who I knew would appreciate her, even though my jealous wife would not, and besides, she was simply too beautiful to resist. I caught and returned a couple more cutthroat on the Henry's Hopper, just for the sake of anticlimax, and drove home in a self-satisfied daze, having answered no questions except for the one all anglers ask: "Wonder what they're bitin' today?"

Ignorance

Lance Olsen

When travel author and novelist Mary Morris debarked from
the pygmy plane at the Pullman-Moscow Airport one cold
oyster-gray spring day in 1996, ready to teach in the University of
Idaho's Distinguished Visiting Writers program for two
weeks, she carried under her arm the March issue of *GQ* with a
dumb photo of a simpering David Schwimmer sporting a
lipstick smooch on his lower left cheek on the cover, and an even
dumber article inside titled "A Journey to the Heart of
Whiteness" about what it called "Fascistville, Idaho." The piece
was obese with black-and-white photos of the jowly
seventy-eight-year-old Reverend Richard Butler giving a Hitler
salute on the front steps of his Church of Jesus Christ
Christian near Hayden Lake, a biker chick named Geo (as in short
for "Georgia") blowing up a condom for laughs like a balloon
beside what looked like her bearded logger boyfriend, and these
Stepford-like tow-headed kids in white shirts and black
ties that were just too creepily clean for their own good; and it
asserted things like "The lovely lake region of northern
Idaho is home to the Aryan Nations, Mark Fuhrman and a
cracked pot of other white supremacists united by hate.
African-Americans, Hispanics and Jews are not welcome here. It
is, its residents boast, what America used to be—and must
be again."

You get the picture. Mary Morris arrived thinking she had it all figured out. She'd done her homework. Now all she had to do was cool her heels in aloof, single-eyebrow-raised cosmopolitan amusement of us back-country folk, taking mental notes for some knee-slapping anecdotes she'd be able to tell her buddies back in New York when she returned. You could see it all over her face. She showed that issue to everyone she met as if it were some sort of passport to the good life.

I felt really embarrassed for her, especially with her being a pretty well-known travel writer and all. What sort of homework was this? So I determined to make it my overzealous business to show her she'd been duped by a bad media construct in chic's clothing. Just as the South has been metaphorized through beautifully gruesome novels like James Dickey's *Deliverance,* which looks back to those by Faulkner, which look back to Poe's stories, to stand in for our nation's collective id, so, too, Idaho in particular and the Inland Northwest in general have been metaphorized by CNN and its ratings-hoggish sound-byte clowder to stand in for our nation's angry ignorant political extremism, for life on the crazy brink. Idaho, outside of Idaho, is nothing more than the blond leading the blond. It's nothing but a bunch of underwashed, jowly, condom-inflating survivalists, supremacists, freemen, tax resisters, home schoolers, militia members, right-to-lifers, libertarians, Christian patriots, and O'Boise potato chips.

It probably goes without saying that bromidic preconceptions die fairly hard, particularly when there's some gnat's eyebrow of truth to them. It took some industrial-strength effort on my part, not to mention a visit to the town bar-cum-diner in Helmer (population way below thirty), on the way to Bovill, and a four-wheel excursion over snowy Mica Mountain with seven people from the University, one of them Steve Banks, novelist Russell Banks's brother (Russell a good friend of Mary's), and two weeks in a classroom full of sweet talented open-minded students, to convince Mary I'd never seen any of the crack-potted above, not a single one, during my eight years in this state, that I've heard the Aryan compound south of Sandpoint boasts something like a majuscule six families, and that I didn't behold my first potato till this spring, when my artist wife, Andi, and I planted eighteen of them in our garden just to suss out what they really looked like anyway, and discovered they flourished in this soil and climate like weeds on a sunny summer day along the Jersey Turnpike.

Mary Morris's initial reaction, in all fairness, is easy enough to understand. The fact is most people find it almost impossible to squint through the televisual and journalistic prefab fog to the thing itself. Electronic hype is heady stuff at this early date in a new millennium. Plus most people have virtually no clue where Idaho actually resides—except, perhaps, as a vaguely disconcerting mis-manufactured state of mind. My nephew, Matt, for example, who lives in Austin, phoned recently and offered to drive up and stop in a couple of days on his way to college at the University of Chicago. I explained we'd be only too happy to have him, but that he'd be detouring a few thousand miles out of his way in the process. He explained, after a nonplused pause, that he assumed since the first letter in our state's name was "I," it had to be somewhere in the Midwest, close to Iowa, Indiana, and Illinois, where all such states resided by clear alphabetical decree. Which is just a little strange, no doubt, but comprehensible given Matt's junior age. What isn't comprehensible is how, when Andi and I moved here from our jobs at the university in Lexington, Kentucky, in the spring of 1990, our friends on the east coast stopped writing and calling us. Living in Kentucky was bad enough, for goodness' sake, their taciturnity seemed to say, but willfully setting down roots in Idaho was like falling off the flat earth smack into dragon-ridden oblivion. We assured them the postal service and phone lines extended this far west, but they remained dubious for quite some while, reminding us that the adjective most frequently applied to the Northwest by non-Northwesterners was "remote." When they finally relented, they began addressing their letters through some eerie psychological dyslexia to *Dreary*, ID, instead of *Deary*, where we happen to live. Which situation is limpid as an unmuddied stream compared to the reaction of our friends in Seattle, who still treat the world on the eastern side of the Cascades as the American version of Conrad's Congo. I half suspect they expect us to show up on their porches on our next visit in tribal headgear, spears in hand.

I'm probably beginning to sound a little like I'm cooling *my* heels in aloof, single-eyebrow-raised, rural-wise amusement at them there city folk, but I'm not, exactly. A part of me counts a part of me among them. After all, I'm the guy who for the first six months on our farm here carried the shotgun with me out to the barn to dump garbage after dinner just in case a stray cougar should try anything funny. And a corner of me deeply empathizes with my sister Marlette and her husband, Wayne, who came up for a visit last summer. We took them on a walk across our back eighty and I swear Marlette looked clumsy as Neil Armstrong trying to navigate the lunar surface. I couldn't help myself. After a while I asked her what the matter was. "The concrete-to-green ratio is completely out of whack around here," she said, stepping gingerly. Which puts me in mind of our neighbor Homer Ailor's story about the experientially challenged hunters from out east who showed up at his doorstep one autumn to ask when the deer turned into elk.

Why shouldn't we go along with everyone else and imagine Idaho as the end of the earth? It's the image our own media apparatus tries to foist upon the rest of the country—Boise's very suburban, very tidy middle-class presence to the contrary. Go to the county courthouse in Moscow and you'll find the corridors flagged with historical photos that suggest a connection with the past that is, at best, tenuous these days, at worst goofily idealized and mythologized. There's one of Troy's wide main street, dubbed Huff's Gulch back then, and a gaggle of cowboys on horseback wielding their six-shooters above their heads as if prepping to mosey into a scene in a John Wayne film. The photo's about ninety years old, as I remember, from an era when seventy-something Homer Ailor can still recall the spring Indian migrations that skirted his cattle ranch. What we like to recollect about our thirteenth-largest state is that it holds the most wilderness of the lower forty-eight: it still houses a smidgen over a million people at a moment when twenty-two-square-mile Manhattan is pushing nine million, nearly a hundred years after the Lower East Side packed in nearly four hundred thousand to its few blocks of tenements...that's ten feet per person, roads and sidewalks included. But we're as content to forget as the guy who wrote the *GQ* article is content to remember that only 9,365 of those smidgen over a million are Asian, according to the 1990 census, only 3,370 black. We're nothing if not strangers in a strange land.

Still, some of us are all too happy to cash in on our bogusly defined status as foreigners in those metropolitan eyes of New York publishers, a distant echo of those "exotics" brought back to Europe from "The Dark Continent" in the sixteenth century to keep the Elizabethan court tickled. Sometimes it seems to me no one can escape Idaho's fabled gravitational force to tell its honest story to the outside world, and sometimes it seems to me that's the way we Idahoans kind of like it. At the end of the day, after all, we're the people who cherish the tradition of Vardis Fisher's overcooked prose, stick-figure characters, creaky plots, and muddy mind while tending to overlook that Idaho is also responsible for producing or nurturing some of the truly megalithic modern and postmodern writers and artists...not only Papa Hemingway, our state's literary broken record who with Gertrude Stein's help reinvented the sentence and our twentieth-century existential sensibility, but also Ed Kienholz, simply one of the most important, influential and sui generis international assemblage artists, who lived and died— mostly unacknowledged by Idahoans, while a star in every major city from L.A. to Berlin—in an artists' compound he bought, built, and populated, up near Hope.

Emblematic of such figures is, of course, Ezra Loomis Pound, the *real* pioneer from this state. No one could argue anything other than that his politics were as extreme, mean-spirited, and morally wrecked as Reverend Richard Butler's. Set, game, match. But that comes dangerously close to being beside the point, considering he almost single-handedly conjured literary modernism while living in London during the twentieth-century's teens, exerting terrific influence on Yeats, Eliot, William Carlos Williams, Marianne Moore, Hart Crane, Archibald MacLeish, and e.e. cummings, while

helping Joyce find a publisher for *Ulysses,* engineering Robert Frost's
leap into print, and encouraging D.H. Lawrence and Ford Madox
Ford. All this, and yet the white-boarded, pared-down, analog-for-
an-Imagist-poem house in which he was born on October 30, 1885,
in Hailey (the first house, by the by, to sport plastered walls in the
town) is unmarked, overgrown, unknown among many of Hailey's
inhabitants, and almost impossible to find without the aid of Cort
Conley's careful directions in *Idaho for the Curious.*

Now *that* should be *genuine* cause for state-wide mortification if
anything should, the University of Idaho's spectacular collection
of three-hundred-plus works related to Pound notwithstanding.

William Douglas, the fourth duke of Queensberry, was entertaining
once at his villa in Richmond. The place flaunted a fabulous view
of the Thames. His guests couldn't get enough of it, and continued
churning out compliment after compliment about the river. After
a while, Old Q, as his friends called him, had heard more than
enough about matters other than himself. He just couldn't contain
his chagrin. "What is there to make so much of in the Thames?"
he burst out. "I am quite tired of it. Flow, flow, flow, always the
same." I'm sure there are many inside and out of Idaho who feel
similarly about our fluvial state, given the simultaneously
homogeneous and radically conflicted image of it presented by
internal and external essayists, reporters, fiction writers,
photographers, fanatics, travel writers, and so forth. Only the
reality remains, Old Q's claim to the contrary, that no two rivers
are the same, no two stretches of the same river, no one stretch
at different instants of the day or month or year. And every river
is nothing if not a manifestation of the myriad streams that nurse
it, each with its own distinct fluent genetic code.

I came to consciousness in a jungle compound, a flat-roofed cement
block of a structure surrounded by twelve-foot-tall Cyclone
fencing topped with barbed wire, near the thick sluggish brown
Amazon in Venezuela, where my father helped launch an oil
refinery. So much of me is in that river, though I don't recall ever
having seen it. What I do recall is checking my shoes in the

muggy mornings for scorpions, my bedding in the muggy night for snakes, the crunch of crabs under our car tires during the rainy season, the snort of a wild boar on the other side of that fencing one afternoon, the downright military might of bugs in the bush that once sprayed my father's face with acid as he macheted his way...and then, in a sort of phenomenological quantum leap, a temporal whitewater sinkhole, strolling along the weed-thick banks of the sour-smelling Hackensack River in River Edge, New Jersey, on my weekly walk to the hermetically sealed, climate-controlled malls where I grew up...and hurrying along the shore path of the electric-blue confluence of streams and agricultural runoff called Lake Mendota in Madison, Wisconsin, where I colleged, on my daily walk to class on a campus where the sixties didn't get around to giving up the ghost till the late seventies, and where tear gas sometimes collected around my ankles dense as nineteenth-century London smog in the mornings...and hustling along the deceptively still Iowa River that always pulled a few students into its malignant currents every year while it apparently tortoised its course through Iowa City where I workshopped, on my biweekly sojourn to the Student Union for a warm drink on a forehead-searingly cold winter's day when there was nothing to do *except* write...and then wading with my Andi beneath the waterfall that abruptly erupted over smooth boulders in an unnamed brook in the Shenandoah National Park outside of Charlottesville, Virginia, in the Blue Ridge, where we knocked around on breaks from work on my dissertation there...and, maybe most important, padding with her, during our frequent stays, along the concrete banks of the Thames itself, the wide silver strip of foil winding through my favorite megalopolis, dropping and rising by the height of a house from tide to tide, flowing a hundred-meters-per-minute, proving every minute just how wrong poor Old Q really was.

The danger in talking about rivers, though, is that before too long you find yourself kissing a mouthful of clichés. It's disconcertingly easy to neglect Old Q's unintentional lesson and clay them all into one great gray literary lump, or, worse, commence making symbols from their physics, metaphors from their hydraulics. Rivers aren't Time, however much poets and prophets wish they were, and they

aren't Life, and they aren't Memory, and they aren't The Great
Feminine, and they aren't Spiritual Sanctuary, and they aren't
Nature Writ Large. They are, well, rivers. They are lots of waters
and not just a few rocks. Aesthetically gorgeous water and rocks,
mind you, but water and rocks nonetheless. I'm tempted to wax
rhapsodic about my experiences among the ones in Idaho—my
first jaw-dropping rafting trip down the River of No Return, say,
understanding with the first splash and bump and drop that
existence would never much improve on this; or the way the middle
falls near Elk River sort of sneaks up on you as you hike toward
it...distant rumble, then subway thunder, then, *whoosh,* trees
parting and the expansive panorama of blue-greenly pined
mountains bobbing all the way to the horizon, the colorful mist of
spring flowers glissading down the slopes toward the black water
forever turning foam-white, and launching. I'm tempted, but I
won't. Why should I? What's the point? I don't feel up to the job
today, and I won't feel up to the job tomorrow. I know the limits
of my language: how do you describe a July sunset around here
without making it sound like one of those velvet paintings sold
along sidewalks in Venice Beach? And I know how much more up
to the job so many others who live in this state are. Bill
Studebaker, I'll be the first to admit, can kayak me right under
the waves. Bob Wrigley can name fifty birds before I've spotted
even one. Ron McFarland can fish me into trout-lush limbo. I'm
the kind of guy, for better or worse, who needs an experienced
guide to enter a small boat made of dark blue rubber, who feels
like a cheat when applying some used human syllables to a circling
hawk. I'm the kind of guy who as a kid fished often, though never
with a hook; I took precautions so I might avoid the misfortune of
actually catching something.

If the truth be known, I don't even know the name of the river I
want to write about in this essay. This isn't because I don't have
one in my head, I hasten to add, or haven't contemplated the topic
a great deal before sitting down at my word processor. It's because
I conceive of my project, right here, right now, as being a good
deal more modest than that. I don't feel tall enough to try to
capture the Selway or Payette in prose. Maybe someday I will, but

I doubt it. For me Bear Creek, the yard-wide stream that flows out
of Mica Mountain, across our back property for forty acres, and
then off to the River Gods know where, is more my size. That's
my connection to the fluviatic these days.

Andi and I flew into the Pullman-Moscow Airport one oyster-gray
April day in 1990 in the same sort of pygmy plane Mary Morris
would use six years later. I'd gotten tired of my job in the
teeth-grittingly conservative English department at the university
in Lexington, and decided to toe the market to see just how
cold it really was. It was plenty cold, let me tell you. It was downright
frigid. But one afternoon I happened upon an ad for a position in
creative writing and contemporary fiction at the University of
Idaho that looked a good deal like it had been penned with me in
mind. Before flying out for the on-campus interview in late
February, I'd never been to the Northwest. All I took with me was
an image of the dark green that shaded most of the state on the
map in my *World Book* encyclopedia, copyright 1966, and a lovely
description of the area authored by the former department chair. I
fell for the space of the place immediately, the sparse population,
the shocking sense for this New Jersey boy of being able to
stand in front of Bob Greene's BookPeople in Moscow and look
north up Main Street and see one end of town and the rolling
hills of the Palouse beginning to tumble away like some corner of
Scotland, and look south down Main Street and see the other
end of town and the rolling hills of the Palouse beginning to tumble
away like some other corner of Scotland; and I fell for the way
there weren't any parking meters to be found, and the way most
people didn't lock their cars or houses, and the way they stopped
and talked to their acquaintances as they walked along the brick-
buildinged downtown on errands; and I found the English
department, for the most part, just as friendly, supportive, and
almost weirdly receptive to my eccentric takes and tastes on
eccentric subjects ranging from cyberpunk to critical theory and
narrative craft to the advent of a then-rough digital beast called
hypertext. During my short stay, I reported back to Andi from the
front lines via phone every three or four hours, trying out a whole
bunch of those used human syllables to capture the feel of this

special district of the imagination while intuiting all too palpably the weight of responsibility that went along with such a task.

When everything was said and done, however, we both knew we were home. When we flew in on that oyster-gray April day in that pygmy plane, it was to locate a place to live. Our hollow-cheeked finances being what they were, we'd given ourselves exactly three days to execute this chore. We arrived assuming we'd rent a modest apartment for a year or two while in the meantime looking for something a little more substantial some decompressive distance out of town. Instead, we ended up teaming with a terrific realtor named Shelley Bennett, who the next day took us to view, among three or four less startling possibilities, a small log house about twenty-five miles northeast of Moscow. It had been built by the owner, Pat Tyndall, and had taken him a long eleven years to finish. Pat worked for the phone company. Each time he was paid he invested into supplies whatever money was left after all the uninteresting disbursements. He constructed the place by hand, his only helpers his two sons. Each weekend he'd drive out from Moscow, where he lived in a duplex, to the pastures and pines that undulate down to Bear Creek four miles southwest of Deary, a bantam town of five hundred (on a good day when everyone's home) founded in 1899 by an Irish-Canadian logger named Bill, on the Joe Blailock homestead, and cogitate and chop, saw and hammer.

The result of his labors was a marvelous invention; upstairs a large sloped-ceiling bedroom leading onto a large sloped-ceiling loft, on the ground floor a room for writing, one for reading, a diminutive living room spilling into a diminutive kitchen, all dominated by a hulking flat-black wood-burning stove, the only source of heat in winter, and a stuffed black bear perpetually rearing up in the attack position (which Pat later gave us as a house-warming present, before striking out for northwestern Montana) he claimed to have shot by himself because it was molesting cattle in the neighborhood, but which, we later and less heroically learned, had in actuality been baited by Pat and then shot by his unnerved wife when Pat had wandered into the woods to relieve himself. In the unfinished basement was plenty of room for Andi's art studio. The

month Pat tacked the last trim to the sweet-smelling pine walls
inside, and finished the railing on the unassuming deck out back,
his wife filed for divorce, his first son entered the special forces,
and his second ran away.

And, of course, we showed up with Shelley Bennett. The spring
drizzle had clouded over the Chinese hat of Potato Hill to the east
and the swelling spine of Mica Mountain to the north.
Everything hovered in a smoke-blue mist and the land appeared
to flatten itself out. But Pat was undaunted. He was intent on
showing us the back property, and we were intent on seeing it. We
climbed into his banged-up lipstick-red Ford pickup and,
windshield wipers clacking, four-wheeled into the gully behind his
house and up across the soggy gray-green pasture and right
to the barbed-wire fence that divided it from the woods hilling
down to the creek. A couple of minutes, and we were pausing,
hands in the pockets of our down vests, among a stand of young
ponderosa beside a large fallen spruce. Suddenly Pat couldn't help
himself. His eyes sparkled and Shelley cringed. For some
reason he had to show us the spot where a hunter sat the season
before to retie his left boot and received a stray bullet smack
in his surprised forehead. Some college kids had been cruising in a
pickup on a gravel road nearly half a mile away when they'd
spotted five deer foraging at the edge of the woods in which we
now stood. One kid got his rifle from the rack and slid out
and fired three times at the buck. Two of the bullets missed the
hunter, who proved to be a relative of Homer Ailor's, but
the third bit him. Hard. The kid hadn't been drinking. He was
apparently a good shot. Except somehow he'd forgotten
about using a backdrop when aiming, and this just impressed the
hell out of Pat. He told us the story twice, as if maybe we hadn't
fully appreciated it the first time. I remember how sweet
everything smelled at that instant, the moist air dense with humus
and pine needles, and I remember looking over Pat's shoulder
down to Bear Creek as he began to tell the story once more.
I didn't know then that Bear Creek could, swollen with melting
snow from Mica Mountain, widen in the early spring from its
current quiet three-foot width into a rushing riverine forty, eighty,

sometimes even a hundred yards back there, filling the meadow between two hills and, maybe a mile on, washing out four or five times a season the bridge that connected us with the Troy Highway, shapeshifting the landscape a little with each occasion, shipping off this downed tree, erasing that small white-sand beach, nudging into being this other one. Nor did I guess that, three years later, during the worst drought in decades, it could evaporate completely, leaving a dry pebbly bed where you could find, if you turned over some of the more rotund rocks, nests of crawfish clustering together blindly. I didn't know we'd adopt Daisy, either, the fawn Pat nursed back to health after a coyote ambush, and Roxy, the raccoon Pat gave us after running over its mother one night, or that Andi and I would hike down to Bear Creek with them on warm summer days in some nigh-biblical procession and take our boots off and soak our feet in the icy water and feed Daisy the crackers and apples we'd brought with us while Roxy nosed around along the grassy banks and picked up small unidentifiable things she discovered in her tiny long-nailed human hands and gnawed at them, investigating, head raised as if in contemplation. I didn't know that three years later bark beetles would descend in another nigh-biblical operation upon those woods and that to stop their progress we'd have to cut down more than a hundred trees from which we'd take our five-cord each summer to get us through the winter; or that Daisy, herself having had two sets of twins, wouldn't make it through one of the harshest winters, snow nearly six feet deep and night temperatures thirty below, the only mode of transportation around the property for us snowshoes and cross-country skis, and that another neighbor, Danny Griffin, Homer's son-in-law, would find what was left of her after spring thaw; or that Roxy, grown, would set off on her own two years after that and then return nearly eighteen months later for a visit in the middle of the night, fat as an ursine cub, minus a toe, plus a brood of her own; or that Andi would slip on her skis while trying to cross a frozen Bear Creek and bruise her shin bone so badly it would still reveal a lump to the touch in June; or that we would picnic among thousands of wildflowers on the hillside with my mother during her summer visits, unaware that cancer was already growing inside her right breast and gliding in a malignant flotilla through her system like autumn leaves on running water.

But I knew enough. I made a point of learning what I needed to learn, always making sure to save enough room in my consciousness for a good swath of flat-out, wide-eyed, ever-delighting ignorance. I learned, while Daisy was alive, how to post our road with no-hunting signs. When the third tree I tried to cut creaked and sat back on my chain saw, bending the blade almost into a right-angled joke and sending the thing up five or six feet into the air, I learned to talk to someone in the forestry department and find out how to do this loud business right, and when in the first light snow of our first light winter I decided to pass on buying studded tires and see how far I could go without four-wheel drive, then skidded off the highway, barely missing an oncoming logging truck, and rolled our Geo Tracker into a ditch, Andi sitting beside me Viking-erect the whole interminable time, I learned what it took to motor along safely out here during the hardhearted months.

Yet not a whit more. Not a mite. I've always reserved a table in the restaurant of ignorance for me and mine. Why? Because there is ignorance, and then there is ignorance. Because sometimes it's better, at least given my hard wiring, to know less instead of more about certain subjects. Because there's mean-spirited, closed-brained, unwholesome unenlightened stuff, and then there's a certain frame of mien that allows us to enjoy some events and things to a greater and greater extent the littler and littler we know about them. Despite the fact I took piano lessons for more years than I can tally, for instance, and despite the fact I played keyboards in a bad rock'n'roll band in high school for two years, dreaming of fame and fans, and can still bang out a belabored rendition of "Crocodile Rock" with the best of them, I never learned the particulars of music, never took the time and effort to commit them to memory. I didn't want to take a chance of letting Bach's *Brandenburg Concertos*, or the songs comprising the second side of the first album I ever bought and ever truly loved, *Sgt. Pepper*, sound anything other than the gates of heaven to me. To that extent, my critical books aside, I'm not a scholar and never will be. I prize benightedness way too much for that.

Not that I haven't tried. Once or twice a year our experientially rich friends, Phil Drucker and Jeannie Harvey, come out for an evening, and before long we find ourselves hiking down by Bear Creek. Phil, a guy with a knock-you-down naturalist's eye and blow-you-over-with-a-feather data base, points to this flower and that tree, naming them with an adoration that rattles me so profoundly I always listen, repeat, and file away the euphonic sonics with gentleness and deference...and, with just as much gentleness and deference, forget them within a week or two. I don't mean to. This isn't a malicious—or even conscious—choice. It's just the way my internal systems operator does merchandising. Someone once asked John Updike what he regretted most in life. He told the interviewer his time as a student at Harvard. "Why?" the interviewer asked, openly perplexed. "Because that's the place that civilized me," Updike answered. As an undergraduate at a much less refining institution, I took an introductory course in theoretical physics that made my heart beat faster than almost any other there except the one in twentieth-century fiction, which I made a point of learning everything I could about. It was taught by a big, bearded, bloated-bellied saint named Robert Marsh in a wide cowboy hat, cowboy boots, and jeans. He'd written the textbook for the class, as well, and I will never forget its last paragraph, which, in pedagogically more optimistic, less chicly cynical times, I used to read to my students on the last day of every semester. "To be human is to wonder," it begins. "Children wonder for a while, before we teach them to be smug about the obvious and to stop asking silly questions. It is easier to pay men to retain a little of the child and do our wondering for us.... I, for one, refuse to believe that nothing can be done about this empty place, or about the more general disease of which it is but a minor symptom. But as long as we are sundered so, let me remain one of the children and wonder."

Wonder is the flip side of ignorance. That, I suppose, is what draws me back again and again to science—or, better, speculative—

fiction, as reader and writer: not that it has all those neat high-tech
gadgets and answers in it, but that it is the only genre that
can instill a true sense of awe in us about the universe and our tiny
blue address in it at a cosmic level. All the rest strikes me as flat
and faded beside it. And that, I suppose, is also what draws me to
rural living, to this farm that Andi and I have taken to calling
"The Monastery," behind closed doors, to those grassy banks
running beside Bear Creek. What in the world can instill you with
a true sense of awe along the cramped homogeneous corridors
of suburbia, or the cramped homogeneous corridors of domestic
fiction that reflects it? How many failing relationships and studies
in victimology can you read about in these days of whine and
posers before it's time to pick up another genre, a different, more
startling and encompassing vision? Cities, perhaps, are another
story, except even Lord Balfour of Burleigh knew back in 1944 that
"London is a splendid place to live for those who can get out of it."
Cities are fine to visit, but who in the world would want to reside
in one? It may be true, as Homer Ailor said of St. Louis before his
first trip to Missouri, that there are more than a million people
inhabiting it, but you don't see them all at once. It's equally true,
however, that the ozone in Washington, D.C., generated during a
recent heat wave through various industrial and auto emissions
tangoing with the incoming UV rays, drove the urban population
indoors for a week and damaged the lungs of those who were
foolish enough not to heed the media's warning for days afterward,
and that the rain in L.A. sometimes possesses the consistency
of low-grade battery acid. Reviewers sometimes complain about
my novels' bleak outlook, what with their frequent focus on
apocalyptic future visions, environmental catastrophe, and
less-than-buoyant appraisal of the human spirit, but living a short
walk from Bear Creek—like reading the great dystopic
speculative fiction by Mary Shelley, Anthony Burgess, Philip K.
Dick, Margaret Atwood, and William Gibson—is a constant
reminder of what's to lose of ourselves and our planet if we're not
careful.

It just may be that besides—or perhaps precisely because of—
their general unpleasantness, cities are well on the road to

becoming obsolete communal constructs; pet rocks of the industrial revolution. Anyone with a good modem, a fair computer, Web-access to Amazon.com books, subscriptions to several newsgroups of choice, plus a satellite dish with some real drawing power no longer needs them as the locus of culture, or even of commerce and trade. It's not that our metropolitan selves are dissolving, nor that we're simply and simplistically turning our backs on cities like some parochialist-masquerading-as-regionalist like Thomas Hart Benton, whose hyperbolic canvases sometimes appear as if they were designed by Walt Disney on downers; who holed up in his bland birthland of the rural Midwest most of his life because he was frightened by the aesthete-minded homosexuals he discovered on his short forays to Chicago, New York, and Paris, delighting in his bucolic comrades-in-pitchforks because they were, as he said, "highly intolerant of aberration." We're not reconstituting the droopy cellulite-ridden City-as-Sodom myth again. Just the opposite. Our millennial selves are cleaving, becoming multidimensional, as comfortable with the speed of the digital beyond as with the early fall Bear Creek, with tugging down Tokyo's or London's newsfeeds from geosynchronous satellites to see what the rest of the global village is up to as with tugging out thistles from the garden, with channel surfing as a mode of consciousness as with a porcupine's creep up a lodgepole. The real question at the launch of the twenty-first century is this: why limit ourselves? Why restrict who we are in terms of selfhood, literary genre, political correctness, living locales, perspectives on the world or off it? Many short-sighted critics, committed to short-term gain at the price of long-term loss, believe the Pathfinder's crawl across Mars was really a wasteful expenditure having to do with sniffing some funnily named rocks. Nothing could be farther from the truth. For the cost of making one awful action-adventure like *Waterworld*, the Pathfinder's mission was all about the most important query of the next hundred years.

When, after decades of searching, you finally come across Bear Creek, or its equivalent, your first instinct is to shut the figurative door behind you. Who doesn't want to be the last person to locate the end of the earth? Who doesn't want to keep the population low there? Almost twenty years ago Mary Leakey discovered footprint remnants crossing seventy-five feet of the arid Laetoli plain of Tanzania. They were 3.75 million years old. Three early members of the human family, three little hominids, had made their journey side by side. From the evidence of their footprints, one had paused and turned left briefly. He or she was the first artist, checking out the road less traveled, and I presume—at least in the topography of my own mythologization of the state— everyone who moves to Idaho wants in some small way to be that personoid: the one who does things just a little differently from most; the odd man or woman out; the one who wants to live and let live in privacy with a certain quiet generosity of spirit. I know, in any case, that I do. I'm afraid I might come to take The Monastery for granted if there are any more people to share it with me. I shudder every time I hear Coeur d'Alene has spread a little farther around one of the most toxic lakes in the country, and I'm beginning to understand my fellow citizens of Deary who feel devastated because town population increased by a cataclysmic fifty people in the ten years between censuses.

Down deep, not only my numerical but also my spatial relationships have modified since first standing on that hill with Pat Tyndall on that drizzly afternoon and looking down at Bear Creek. Presently, if I can ferret out a single farm light at night burning half a mile or a mile down the road from our digs (Andi and I keep ours turned off as a neighborhood courtesy), I feel pinched. A suburban friend of ours came to visit for a week not long ago and experienced instantaneous discomfort at how far away the next house was situated. What about emergencies? What about social intercourse? She was dumbfounded when I explained to her we've begun thinking of moving again because that next house has come to feel so doggone close, and she found herself at a loss for words when I then asked her how many of her neighbors she actually knew, and of those how many she actually cared to know. Sometimes I slip and surprise myself pitying those who pity what they conceive as our solitude. With Bear Creek, a good imagination and a new pen, a bookshelf and an e-mail account, a raspberry patch and a vegetable garden, CNN and MTV, lots of snow to shovel in winter and lots of wood and grass to cut in summer, those indescribable sunsets and a cornucopia of movie channels, the spectacular show of the northern lights and a pretty wide firepit, the buzzing silence of the yard broken only occasionally by a robust breeze or a birdsong, frequent visits by friends and writerly acquaintances, a buffalo ranch down the road in one direction and a cattle ranch and horse ranch in the other, and eighty acres inhabited at different times of year by more deer than you can fit into the space of your mind's eye, coyote moms frisking with their pups on spring afternoons in the meadow, foxes cantering across snowy fields in January, raccoons, farm cats, skunks, owls, and even the occasional thin-legged, freight-train-torsoed moose, how could anyone possibly feel anything except continually surrounded by excellent company?

Shortly after we moved here, Andi and I hit upon the pure plain perfect final touch: a freestanding hot tub. We bought a kit and I learned what I needed to learn to pound together the cedar boards and barrel rings, and sink the top-loading wood-burning stove. We situated the product of my labors a couple hundred yards to the north of our house, in a stand of tall grass and young Austrian pines, perhaps ten feet from that garden I put in and fenced. It took quite a while to compose because I had so much to reckon about what to do and how to do it. You can imagine the sense of satisfaction coursing through me upon completion. We bided our time the rest of that day, and fired up the contraption around eight that night. By ten the water was amniotic warm. We stripped down and shinned in and had a good laugh at our good fortune...and then we looked up. It simply never occurred to me that cities and suburbs had colonized the night, that the best you could possibly get when arching your neck in London was a pink-gray brume, in New York a starless black. Only here...here was an outrush of stellar activity, and if you stared long enough you even began to see pinprick satellites sliding across the star mist, and if you waited long enough you even began to see meteors skid through the atmosphere at a much greater rate than you ever supposed they could, and I realized, as Andi and I sat side by side gazing toward the hazy center of the Milky Way some twenty-seven thousand light years from our silence, that that blurry band of light above us was the only consequential river in Idaho, the night sky the ocean.

The Little Salmon: Confessions at the Edge of the Time Zone

Joy Passanante

Okay, I'll lay this right smack on the desktop and confess: my first river-loyalty is embedded in the Midwest—the Muddy Mississippi, Old Man River, Big River, its legends as long as its string of sobriquets. Born only twelve miles from its dramatic banks down a cobblestone drop from Broadway in St. Louis, I spent twenty years of my life absorbing its lore—fishing with my father, watching him gut the catfish that my mother would reluctantly fry, belting out odes to the Old Man at my suburban elementary school and Camp Zoe in the Ozarks. And learning respect, in school and out, for this Mighty force, the longest river in the U.S.—2,348 miles— one that delineates the boundaries of ten states. I know, I know, heresy for an Idahoan, even an adopted one.

Certainly one of the highlights of my tenderer years was the excursion that my mother arranged for my little sister, Judy, and me on the riverboat, *The Admiral.* We garnered oohs and aahs in matching midnight blue velvet skirts and silk blouses with Peter Pan collars, Judy roundfaced and dimpled, her dark hair in two thick ponytails arching out from the temples—quintessential fifties. As the white ship churned and hooted its way up and down the mocha-hued waters, we sipped Cherry Cokes, while from the bandstand on the top deck our mother pointed out all the hallmarks of the earliest history of the Euro-American West: on

the Missouri side, the spires of the first cathedral inside the
Gateway to the West (Arch-less in those days); nearby the dome
of the Old Courthouse where the Dred Scott decision hurled the
country closer to civil war; and Schwarz Studio, the first taxidermy
establishment west of the Mississippi. On the Illinois side, the
Peabody Coal plant shot out a column of orange sparks; and in
between, Eads Bridge connected east and west, across which my
father as an eleven-year-old toted satchels of bootlegged whiskey
from Illinois for one of his father's sub rosa business ventures.

When the July sun reddened our cheeks, we followed the music of
a jukebox to a lower deck, and to the tunes of Perry Como and
Doris Day danced the rest of the afternoon away, spinning each
other wildly, our skirts swirling around our lace-edged cotton
panties, our shiny black patent cut-out Mary Janes scuffing the
linoleum until we fell down dizzy and giggling (something we're
still known to do).

In the unwieldy days of junior high, I survived my First Date in
the same place, with Todd Green, a boy who had lived in my
parents' subdivision since we moved from St. Louis city to county,
and who in grade school used to race toward me from the line of
boys on their side of the gymnasium wall to choose me as his square-
dance partner. His parents drove us all the way downtown to *The
Admiral* in their Buick Riviera and then diplomatically disappeared
to leave us alone—feeling vulnerable and, oddly, trapped in the
current bound for New Orleans. While my adolescent date and I
fox-trotted and cha-cha'd on what was now a parquet dance floor
lit with soft-colored lights, the dancing this time stiff and predictable,
and I flailed around like a caught catfish for words that might make
him feel good about himself and me, I wistfully conjured up the
pleasure of my look-alike sister's giggle and grasp in the same place
a decade before. When the band took a break we squeezed into a
photo booth in the arcade and bought four flashes for twenty-five
cents. I still have the snapshots, in a column shaped like a bookmark,
each pose one-inch-by-one-inch, recording the straps of the polished
cotton and organza dress I had worn to a Bar Mitzvah the Saturday
before, my tight pin curls and his bow tie, our uncertain smiles.

THE LITTLE SALMON

It is a short lifetime later. Words like "draw," "switchback" and "elk rack," and "eddy," "whitewater rapids," and "shoal" have drifted into my personal lexicon. Although this vocabulary represents a different discourse, rivers for me remain rites of passage, occasions for ceremony. For my fortieth birthday my closest friend of three decades and I rafted the Lower Salmon. My husband and I roasted hot dogs for daughter Liza's first boy–girl party on the dunes of the Snake; toasted daughter Emily's thirteenth birthday on the white beaches of the Lower Salmon; Thanksgivinged on the Lochsa; anniversaried on the Yellowstone; introduced Chinese students to the U.S. riverworld on the Clearwater. When east coast family and friends visit, we head immediately for the Selway or the St. Joe to show off Idaho's star exhibits down to its glittering chips of mica. Moving water is still in my blood—and the sense of occasion that moves along with it.

Among these rivers, the Little Salmon, flowing a mere forty or so miles in the heart of Idaho along the state's major north–south road, has seldom appeared on the list. But I nurture a particular fondness for the Little Salmon and the unlikely, sometimes scruffy bounty of its banks, so different from the monuments up the levees of the Mississippi. The Little Salmon really is that: little. Me, too. Tiptoeing to just five feet, I've always been drawn to the small—doll house furnishings, tiny paper fans, miniature dachshunds, the diminutive cupped petals of lily of the valley. And the Little Salmon, its short stretch from New Meadows to Riggins, is not only small, but as generous with variety as one of those surprise balls, its idiosyncratic little gems wrapped mummylike in layers of crepe paper.

Unlike the Mississippi, which reaches St. Louis from northwestern Minnesota near the Canadian border and empties into the Gulf of Mexico, the Little Salmon courses north. On a breezy June day, armed with curiosity and a cooler, I gas up the Camry and drive south from my home in Moscow until I get to New Meadows, then backtrack to trace this river from as close to its genesis as I can get in a car.

The headwaters of the Little Salmon, somewhere along Blue Bunch Ridge, drain down the West Mountains above New Meadows. The still-teeny river skirts the town to the west, but there's a barn with a broken roof that, for me, marks the actual spot, which is too distant to see from the highway. Already, before it winds into New Meadows, it has taken on two or three creeks, reinventing itself several times over. (On my way north I count close to twenty of them; within the first few miles Threemile Creek, Fourmile Creek, Martin Creek, and Sixmile Creek all trickle off the Salmon River Mountains from the east.) The joined waters curlicue, continuing to receive streams, and meander around an expanse of meadow. Vistas are broad. Cattle graze bucolically. (To celebrate these moments, I plug Beethoven's *Sixth Symphony—The Pastoral*—into the tape deck.) We cross the forty-fifth parallel, the little river and I—another Significant Event. It marks the place halfway between the equator and the North Pole, and there's a momentary sense of suspension, of perfect balance, and all this somehow recalls the Mississippi, separating east from west in the America of earlier frontiers, and my earlier rites of passage, in St. Louis, where Lewis and Clark launched their voyage to…hmm, around here, actually.

As I contemplate these connections, the river runs by a trendy settlement of varnished log homes, a hallmark of the chic New West, where it obligingly waters the green of a meticulously groomed golf course. But suddenly at the far end of the meadow, the cattle vanish, a new stream spills down from the west, the tamaracks close in, and I draw in breath as I would at the skyward arc of a Ferris wheel as the road begins to descend and the gathering of waters abandons its placid flatland loops to rip straight into a canyon of white rock. In this stretch Highway 95 crosses and recrosses the stream. The water swells at Hazard Creek, where, abruptly, whitecaps bubble over blanched boulders—and presto!—a bona fide river.

The human landscape changes, too. Isolated ramshackle houses stranded on piles of mud-caked rock from the river's rampage of February 1997 create their own islands. The river whooshes by abandoned motels on the left, Fall Creek Café ("closed on Monday," the sign says, but I've never seen it open on any day of the week), rusted trucks, junked washers and dryers and refrigerators in front of Dave's Repair close to Pinehurst, clusters of house trailers with tin roofs, chicken coops, and satellite dishes dwarfing the buildings. (If I had a Loretta Lynn tape, I'd replace the Beethoven.) The canyon widens and starts to look more like ranch lands—dried grasses and boulders, dotted with tenacious succulents. The river takes on the sage tones of the hills; smooth river rocks, striped and flecked, shimmer with mica.

The bear-paw hills signal my approach to Riggins, bringing oddly lush roses, peach trees. Rapid River runs into the Little Salmon about four miles above its mouth. On the left bank is an auto graveyard, stacks of crushed cars. Cottonwoods puff up fluff. I whiz by the turnoff to the Seven Devils, Hells Canyon Ranger Station, and the last creek: Squaw. The river and I enter Riggins (pop. 555, if you include Lucile—together they constitute the metropolis of the Little Salmon), the self-proclaimed "Whitewater Capital of the World." The confluence of Salmons at the site of the old mill in Riggins is masked by such establishments as Cattleman's Café and the Salmon River Inn, whose menu items feature sandwiches named after the rapids on the River of No Return and "Hard Ice Cream." (I smile at this remnant of the macho West.) I like to think of this place, my favorite of Idaho communities, as a rough-and-tumble cowboy town with a proto-chi-chi tourist mentality. So far, it's still what I think of as "the real Idaho." (When a couple of years ago I noticed the advent of an advertisement for "espresso" at the Stinker station, I groaned.)

Lots of surprises for such a little guy of a river, quirky and eclectic. But it remains a river that doesn't take over the conversation, or focus the vision overmuch, a backdrop river. In spite of its fitful ripping through the canyon, it isn't at heart theatrical. Not overdramatic so as to upstage my inner vision. In short, it provides a good place to write.

In the West, where the land itself is history enough, and the impulse to prove our rugged inner selves against the spectacle of the scenery is more historical fact than cliché, we have to think hard to come up with fresh myths for ourselves. For me, this is the spot, less than a mile from this confluence of Salmons, where Pacific flows into Mountain Time, where I choose to hide out, retrench. Here I can wade in my private myths, dip into metaphor, sweep down the current of the subconscious. Okay, so I get carried away, but it works.

I coast down the slope into the Lodge B and B, to the cabin I rent by the week. Just two months earlier, a colleague of mine found himself a few miles from here slugging it out with some river drifters and was sent back up north with a concussion and fractured jaw. Knowing this, I come anyway, and alone. When I reenter the world of the Little Salmon, it is to be in some ways vulnerable, in the way of all writers, to let whatever muses we can muster pitch their tents and do their stuff.

The cabin is wedged between the highway and the river ten feet from its edge. It's a single room crammed with beds and throw pillows, but there's enough space for me to pace and jive around to my taped music. One wall is completely covered by a paper mural of the Alps. (Ironically, if a window were cut through the same wall—and I had a telescope that penetrated the Riggins hills—I'd be able to see the Seven Devils themselves, looking every bit as momentous and striking.)

The first thing I always do is rearrange the furniture. I move the table that will become my desk in front of one of two long windows that afford river views, open it wide to let in the generous sound of the water, stretch my cord to the max to set up the computer as close to the window as possible. One (blessedly narrow) window faces Highway 95; I shut its blinds tight.

☙☙☙

The river's rush blocks out the world of Riggins and its gas stations and bars and realtors and outfitter and rafting companies—and 150 miles away, the world of university students and concerts and libraries and e-mail; and more than two decades away, the land of electric garage doors and Cuisinarts that I left back in the Midwest burbs. In this faux-paneled cubicle of my own, I don't so much write as collect details—scraps to use later. Eventually. Any day now. But now, there's time for laziness. The idiosyncrasies of the river and its banks give me a hodgepodge of goods I can arrange later—hand-jigsawed bits I can take away and—soon, I swear it—smooth out the splinters.

From the chair repositioned to face the window, I watch. A magpie, its wings glossed blue and black, toddles along the cut lawn between me and the river. Redwing blackbirds hover around the tops of poplars. On the hillside across the water, a raccoon lumbers through the brush and yellow blooms (wild daisies? buttercups?). Cottonwood puffs waft by like desultory snowflakes. The view and sound hypnotize me, so that I have to keep myself from becoming agoraphobic, not even wanting to venture out for the blackberry cobbler at This Old House Restaurant, a short walk through locusts and fruit trees at the RV park.

Into the afternoon I watch helicopters make mysterious drops on the cliff across the river; their noise is disconcerting, out of tune with the roar behind me, but intriguing. I imagine guns for militia types, hospital supplies for survivalists. Riggins is a good place to hide, but I am determined to feel everything except fear. After all, I am in a contained place within a contained part of the larger Salmon River system.

That night, the mesmerizing river-voice keeps me asleep, one of its more pragmatic charms against my congenital insomnia. But I leave the curtains open, so that if I do wake I will see the moon-tinted crests undulating.

On the third night of my sojourn, I wake with a start to an unnatural noise—the screeching of heavy machinery, squeaks, and gruff voices—a light out the highway window not there before. I wonder if I bothered to lock the door, and don't want to walk to find out until I throw on a shirt, which is on the other side of the cabin. But my curiosity wins out, and I inch open the blind, letting in a stripe of the sickly yellow light from the highway. A few feet from my window there's a United Van Lines truck the length of an Olympic field spanning the distance from my cabin to the main house and wedged between the road and my door. The driver seems to be having trouble avoiding the phone wires so he can park. He doesn't give my window a glance, and eventually his awkward mechanical antics bore me back to sleep.

But when the sun's out, so am I; I slip the disk into the laptop, take it outside, and set up. I spread a beach towel at the water's edge, where chicken wire holds back small boulders under a concrete wall my landlords have fashioned to keep the Little Salmon's power at bay. Don headphones and plunk in a Linda Ronstadt tape. Sit down to write. Time and water pass by swiftly, and looking at the nonsensical letters on the computer screen I'm just about to wonder if I have something in common with Jack Nicholson's character in *The Shining*, looking at his typewriter and repeating over and over, *All work and no play*, when I sense someone's presence behind me.

I pretend not to notice for a while, but then a giant shadow on my towel makes me remove my headphones. I look up—WAY up—into the sun at the flash of a silver tooth high above my head. It glints—it actually does—and I feel I'm caught on the set of a movie gone amuck—Clint Eastwood meets Bladerunner.

"I'm sorry if I'm interrupting you," the mouth around the tooth begins; the metal gleams front and center. He's sorry? Not many times have I heard these words from a man, especially a stranger, not to mention one with a tattoo of a spread-winged, mean-eyed eagle taking up the better part of one prodigious bicep; a rattlesnake flexed to strike on the other. I put down the laptop. If he had begun "What's a good lookin' lady like you doing with a computer next to a river?" I'd not have repressed my sigh. But something in his voice, even raised artificially over the churning of the water, begs my attention. Gets it.

My gaze swoops down, past the tattoos and glinting tooth, at a small, portly, white critter at the end of a leash next to him, poking around his ankles.

"Got these in Nam." (I realize he's talking about his tattoos, not the animal or the ankles.) "Got my wife there, too. She's in the house." He nods in the direction of my hosts next door.

I change the subject, finding it safer to talk to the animal. "Hello there, fella," I say, stretching out my hand toward the tethered companion, who waddles away. Must be one of those house-pigs, I decide.

"It's a girl. She's a Chihuahua."

Surprise. I arch my brows and notice not only pointy ears but a diamond-studded collar. (Okay, so maybe it's rhinestone.) He continues, "Poor old girl just gained a little too much weight while I make my long hauls and don't have time to stop." The dog clearly resembles a piglet with an old hog's gait.

"What's her name?"

"Misty," he says.

I am expecting something a tad more, uh, manly from a trucker with rattlesnake tattoos—Spurs? Buck? Even Ralph.

"And my sister's dog—" he nods towards my benefactors' place—"is named Missy—and the people in the A-frame upriver just a bit, they have a dog named Mystery. And I kid you not." I smile at his neighborly attitude, the out-of-kilter rhetoric. I exit the file, close up the laptop.

"Like I say, sorry to interrupt, but I hope I didn't bother you any last night. I just couldn't get the truck in without taking the phone wires with it. Came to be with my little sister." I recall hearing that June, who rents me the cabin, has just had a death in the family.

"I'm sorry," I say. He can only nod, moist-eyed; I can tell I've opened the floodgates.

"Don't mean to disturb you or anything, but I have to walk Misty every hour or so." He stoops down, and I snap the laptop out of the way. "She's pushing old age. Has problems getting around." He leans slightly closer, adds sotto voce, "With her hips," and I suspect a subtext.

I nod sympathetically, try not to smile. I'm beginning to like the guy. Vintage vulnerable. The type seems to find me even at the edge of rivers. I reach again toward the pooch, who snarls. I back off, respect a rival's jealousy when I see it.

He looks down at my oblong of towel as if he'd like to figure out a way to fit on it with me. I try not to think his thoughts.

Fortuitous, too, since he leads me over the next bend of familiarity as smooth as glass.

"Actually, she has anal problems, but I'm trying to help her by walking her. The vet told me I could give her some medicine to help her." He seems to wait for my reaction; I guess he never had kids. "But I know if I stick my finger in her anus, I'll blow lunch. But I hate to see her in pain. Tears me up."

Who is this guy?

He invites me on a tour of his truck. I accept, curious, and yet there's an undercurrent of danger, the hint that he could, if we were in a slightly different story, shove me into the cavern behind the driver's seat, let loose the brake, and jam down on the accelerator. He has to boost me up, a gesture strangely intimate. Inside it's spacious, and carpeted, and he points out all its attributes with pride—the coffee maker, a bed tightly tucked, a computer with a dot matrix printer.

"I'm gonna tell you something I haven't told many people." I brace myself: from a man who is so open about his dog's nether anatomy, anything could come rolling out. I repress images of a story about slaughtering Vietnamese villagers with a machete. "I write poetry," he says sheepishly.

"Wow," I say, genuinely surprised. And relieved.

"I'm not very good, of course…but—"

"It's not always about being good," I offer, and think of filing that advice away for my dry days.

He smiles gratefully. "You're nice, you know."

I climb down from the cab without his help. He follows. We both stare at the river, but I get the idea he isn't listening to it the way I am.

He says proudly, "I moved a professor once. From Seattle to New Orleans. We got to know each other real well. A little unusual, but the nicest guy you can ever imagine." I am running out of responses. "And he gave me his e-mail address," he adds and waits for me to respond.

I sense a request in the air—perhaps more than one—and let it hover there.

⌒⌒⌒

That night I wait in the lingering edge-of-the-time-zone light until all the bulbs blink out in the house next door. I wrap a towel around me and cross over June and Harvey's deck to the hot tub, which they've graciously invited me to use. I slide its lid toward the perimeter, hoping I can lift it entirely off and on by myself, watch the steam and climb in. I don't turn on the jets; that way I'm immersed in water absolutely still so that I can hear and feel the river instead—more potent by contrast. The moon makes me see in outlines, strips down the complexity. In its glow it haloes a fringe of mountain mahogany that crowns the hill across the river. And then I see him, holding the dog and her leash, murmuring to her in a tongue akin to love, but I know he is looking for me. I wait him out, leave long after the moon has taken its silhouettes and left only a smudgy blue.

In the morning, I stay in bed, thinking. When I hear the door of the truck open, I peek out the blinds facing the highway. Before he hoists himself onto his seat, he lifts the ailing old dog tenderly into the cab, cradling it as if it's a year-old infant, and gets ready to release those massive squeaking brakes to back up the truck and aim it in the direction of Ohio. He glances toward my cabin, holds the gaze and waits for a minute or so, but though it's sunny I stay inside. I'm glad he's left unceremoniously, hasn't blared the horn.

When I walk outside to set up my neat, towel-sized camp again, as close to the river and its concrete-and-rock retaining wall as possible, I find a piece of paper tacked to the door with a small nail. It's a poem, about cowboys, fourteen lines, a sonnet; and I sense the onset of a wild, rootless guilt, for a second wish the river were roaring into my psyche to drown it out. But it's not that sort of river.

⌒⌒⌒

For me rivers are the pulse-pumping backdrop of cameo moments of significance; what I do with them later is up for grabs in the way that what the water does to its beds and rocks, pools and drops, all its inhabitants—and the houses and squatters, neighbors, users, and guests along its bank—is also uncertain. In spite of Old Man River's perennial presence in lore and literature, and his role in the economy and definition of the West, I will instead think of him as a refined old gentleman who assisted me in fixing moments of particular pleasure and awkwardness—kind of like the man with the silver tooth who escorted me into and out of his truck. And the self-contained and odd Little Salmon is a good traveling companion. It may not be a poster river, but it's approachable. Whimsical with a hefty undercurrent of canniness. Giddy at times, though not coquettish. Fretful but not unreasonable.

Despite my insistence on superimposing on wild water myths and metaphors, conscience and cognition, philosophy and fantasy (and I know that, in this, I'm not alone), like all the rivers that call me and stay with me, the Little Salmon—well, it jes' keeps rollin' along.

Two Rivers

Diane Josephy Peavey

My husband squinted then frowned as we flew over Campbell
Dam. Quickly, he circled in the Cessna 182 for a second look. I
followed his glance to the ground below, and, even from our
height, I could see that the rock and dirt wall of the dam had
broken and water was rushing through a hole in the structure.

It was April and we had flown to the ranch to look for signs of
spring, scanning the landscape for the blush of green grasses and
for early runoff. If it looked promising, we would begin the two-
month process of moving five thousand sheep and over a thousand
head of cattle to these mountain meadows from southern Idaho
desert pastures where they grazed over the winter.

At this altitude of 6,000 feet, the snows were just beginning to
melt. We had flown over full lakes and creeks and then to the
Campbell Dam to look at its reservoir that holds water for crops
and livestock during the long, dry summer months, but we had
not anticipated trouble.

We flew back to town where my husband dropped me off and
gathered boots and shovel in his pickup. Without pause, he
retraced our route, this time driving by truck north along the
Little Wood River from the small farming community of Carey.

He told me the story later. The deep mud had made the road to
the dam impassable. Ten miles from town he parked the truck
along the gravel road and began his hike cross country, up and
over a ridgeline. Dragging the long-handled shovel, he pushed and
climbed and pulled himself through sage and rabbit brush in
sucking mud and wet snow, often sinking as deep as three feet on
his three-mile trek to the dam.

There he raced against surging water as he struggled to fill the
hole in the large dirt wall, first with rocks, then with mud packed
around them. When he was done, exhausted and wet, he made the
arduous return trip to his truck.

Despite approaching darkness, curiosity drove him farther into
the ranch to check on Friedman Creek. Only hours earlier from
the plane we had seen the stream contained within the thirty-foot
area of its banks. But now, as he drove up, the waters spilled over
the landscape, easily three hundred yards wide and a foot deep,
blocking the road and flooding the plain.

Frightened by such speed, and suddenly struck by a sense of
foreboding, he turned back, following the road down the farming
valley along the Little Wood River into Carey. In the darkness he
was unaware that he drove only moments ahead of the flooding
waters. He did not know that the river, like its tributaries, was out
of control, and its force had taken out two other dams in a second
drainage. In its springtime fury, it swept trees, willows, and boulders,
some larger than cars, down the road behind my husband. It was
the next morning before my husband learned the extent of the
Little Wood's rage and how he had narrowly escaped with his life.

᭞᭞᭞

My days are shaped by the stories of the Little Wood and its
sister, the Big Wood River. I live part of each year along the banks
of each. I know the communities and their disparate dreams. And
I know that even though they are separated by the narrowest of
ridgelines, they might as well be continents apart in their demands

of their rivers. And in this difference lies the tension of the unsettled landscape in the West, a region at odds with itself where rivers become unwitting central characters.

Their stories are these. Both the Big Wood and the Little Wood flow wild out of rugged central Idaho mountains. While still in the north, each is altered, rechanneled, held in storage dams and reservoirs to serve the needs of the local communities. After running this gauntlet each river flows, notably weakened, across lava rock desert until the two join to form the Malad and then spill into the Snake River of southern Idaho.

But this is the story of the north country, my country, where, after the Big Wood leaves the Boulder Mountains, it moves south through the backyards of multimillion-dollar estates in the ski towns of Ketchum and Sun Valley. Here the river is a kind of ornament for newcomers who arrange its flow to decorate their days.

The community in the Wood River Valley is an oasis of beautiful homes, elaborately landscaped, of the arts, of amenities, outdoor sports, and money. The ski slopes and golf courses are among the best in the country. *The New York Times* is delivered daily so residents can read of the world while they sip their espresso drinks at coffee bars. The grocery stores offer every manner of organic and gourmet food items, for a price. The plethora of gallery owners and music lovers bring in world-renowned artists and performers. Most newcomers understand little of life fifty miles in any direction of this community. If they leave the valley, it is to fly to homes in Los Angeles, New York, Seattle or Chicago.

On the other side of the ridge, the Little Wood flows from the Pioneer Mountains, east of the Boulders, tracing a route south through remote, rural farming and ranching communities, mostly families eking out a living in the arid, high desert landscape. The river is their livelihood. It is a working river, and old-timers write its stories. The people are satisfied to walk the sagebrush landscape and watch seed push up green shoots through newly plowed fields year after year. They run some cattle, a few sheep.

Over coffee in small-town cafes in Carey, Richfield, Dietrich, Shoshone, they talk about the weather and crop prices. If conversation strays to the Big Wood community to the north, they discuss its residents as if a nation of foreigners had settled in their midst. They'll tell you they'd prefer to feel the summer sun from their tractors than from a golf cart any day, although they're not much experienced in the latter. They mostly cut a wide swath around the resorts to the north.

I came to the Big Wood Valley first. It was Christmas and nighttime. I had just driven across the silent, open farming region of the Camas prairie that fills much of the landscape between the Boise airport and the resort community. After turning north on Highway 75, I had headed toward the dark shadows of mountains in the distance. But as I entered the town of Bellevue the evening suddenly was flooded with the holiday season. The glow of colored lights warmed the icy landscape. The air smelled thickly of wood fires.

Over the next few days I explored life along the Big Wood River, driving through the valley with its surprisingly gentle vistas of soft rounded hills and winter-gray sagebrush breaking through the snow. I followed a trail of cars on the two-lane highway, passed a home here, another there, several trailer parks and cabins.

This was not steep Rocky Mountain country, so it was startling to come upon the showpiece ski slope of Bald Mountain with its groomed trails looming at the edge of Ketchum. People came from around the world to ski this mountain and rarely left disappointed. But it was also at the edge of town that the sleepy mood of the valley ended abruptly.

Suddenly everyone was on vacation. Skiers, just off the slopes, wandered in and out of lavishly decorated shops. Eggnog and Christmas sweets were offered along with designer fashions, ski wear, art work or jewelry trinkets. Shoppers fingered extravagant holiday foods in the tinseled aisles of grocery stores while they hummed along to the strains of *Winter Wonderland*. Restaurants and clubs were filled with people in animated après-ski conversation, toasting each other and a new year. All the while, realtors lurked behind their storefront windows, ready to give away the mountains, if necessary, to entice these visitors into permanent holiday homes along the Big Wood.

The resort's glamorous history permeated the area. In the festive lobby of the Sun Valley Lodge, guests scanned the photo gallery of celebrities—Gary Cooper, Ernest Hemingway, Esther Williams, June Allison, Tyrone Power and others. And these personalities stared back from ski slopes or restaurant tables, forever young, forever smiling, forever on vacation at railroad magnate Averill Harriman's grand new ski resort. This splendid playground, rival to any ski area in the world, opened in 1936, and it was here that Harriman pinned his hopes for railroad travel in the West.

Beyond the lodge, in those pre-World War II days, the rest of the valley was almost untouched from the time of the earliest white settlement. Sheep grazed the sagebrush hills and high mountain meadows throughout the summer, and the railroad that brought Hollywood stars to the winter resort shipped huge numbers of lambs to markets around the West in the quiet days of July and August. For a time, the area was second only to Sydney, Australia, as a sheep center.

I saw this rural life in the spring of the year when I drove into Flat Top Sheep Co. for the first time with its owner, the man I would later marry. The heart of the ranch operation was along the Little Wood River, but we stopped at the summit between his land and a neighbor's place, the summit that divided the Big Wood and Little Wood drainage.

The familiar, busy valley was behind us, the town of Bellevue to the west, just out of sight. Ahead of us was a vast expanse of untouched land that extended east from one ridgeline to another into mountain peaks in the distance. I rolled down the window and listened hard to a new kind of silence, one I could almost touch. My friend started to speak. "Shhh," I said. "Shhhh." We listened together.

When we finally drove on, we crossed through open meadows, then passed an old springhouse and stopped to drink from its clear water as pioneer families had done for years. We drove by the sheep corrals and then along the canyon floor beside the Little Wood until we climbed out of the bottoms onto an expanse of hayfields.

We were at the Carey Road junction. We would follow it as it curved east, and travel another six miles to the ranch headquarters. If we had turned south toward Carey, we would have traced the river through the farming valley past the large Little Wood Dam and Reservoir, whose waters sustain local families at the edge of this high desert country. This was the road my husband would drive in the flood of '82.

But we continued east that day into a landscape that opened onto huge meadows stretching into distant sagebrush hills and basalt rock buttes. Cottonwood trees and willows trailed creek banks and wound like ribbons across green meadows. There were fields of tall grasses and fragrant, blooming bitterbrush. My friend stopped to pick a sprig for me. Its strong, sweet fragrance quickly filled the pickup. Deer and antelope raced in front of us and into fields of golden sunflowers and purple lupine. I was stunned by so much space and beauty.

But I was cautious at first and only agreed to spend my summers at this place because the resort community was a short drive away. After all, I was fresh from urban life. The proximity of Sun Valley with its restaurants, bookstores, movies, and coffeehouses seemed a reasonable safeguard against the loneliness of the ranch.

And for years, I kept a foot in both lives. In the summer, I drove over the summit several times a week for groceries and for lunch with friends. In winter, after we moved the animals to pastures in warmer climates, we closed the ranch and my husband and I moved to a small condominium in town. There we'd wait out the snowy months not far from the Big Wood River.

But at the same time I was coming to appreciate that the Little Wood River and its tributaries were the lifeblood of our ranch, of sheepherders, cowboys, dogs, horses, and livestock. Each spring I watched the waters green the pastures and draws that formed the heart of our ranch—Cold Springs, Lake Hills, High Five and the Last Chance. Slowly I became comfortable in this remote country and began counting the days each winter until I could return. In the summer I went to town less often and took a new interest in the work of the ranch.

I learned about roping and branding, gave injections to calves, gathered early newborn lambs from winter snows to warm them under the pickup heater. I rode the desert on horseback behind steers and heifers and cooked for the cowboys on our spring cattle drives. I drove pickups and trailers to winter sheep camps in California. In the late fall I blew on icy fingertips as we herded livestock through chutes for doctoring.

And I began to understand the vagaries of life on the land when we found ourselves in the throes of seven long, silent years of drought. I was stunned to see rushing rivers and creeks disappear into a trickle of water much too early in the summer. I learned the need for local families to join irrigation districts, chart the flow of the Little Wood, and parcel out the water sparingly within the community if the wheat, barley, alfalfa, and potatoes were to grow in years when there was little rain and less snow.

I shared the anxiety of husbands, wives, and children standing on the front porch searching the sky for storm clouds that could break the drought. We, too, stood on our porch and stared into hot blue skies day after day. The animals did not gain weight as usual. We had fewer crops. I became familiar with the columns of numbers that my husband worried over late into the night—budgets, liabilities, assets, commodity prices that didn't compute.

When the drought broke, the families that survived did so because the Little Wood and Big Wood waters were stored in reservoirs and released cautiously until the rains came.

And to my surprise, during those desperate days, I began to turn inward, settling into the silence. This was a life I could not run from. I could not change jobs, move to a new town. This was my home and I hunkered down. And my greatest solace was that the footprint of man was still faint on our ranch lands. Earlier this might have made me lonely but not now. And I realized that friends who came from town to watch the sheepshearing or help move cattle looked longingly at this remote landscape for its secrets, wondering about the sense of their own lives.

It was not surprising they would feel this way. The Big Wood River Valley was changing, expanding, even as I was drawing closer to the land. New housing spilled precariously down the valley along the river. The population of the area tripled. The ski lifts, restaurants, grocery stores now were an extravagance. Many young people who serviced the resort, groomed the mountain after dark, tended bar, and served meals in cafés had moved fifty miles south to find housing they could afford. New large estates lined the banks of the Big Wood despite warnings that that they sat squarely in the flood plain.

And the river, too, had changed. The waters that so intrigued newcomers had been tamed, restrained, confined to make life lovely along its shore. The Big Wood had been channeled and huge boulders pushed in to protect its banks. Its water was used for lawns, landscaping and ponds and to keep the five local golf courses brilliant green. New wells to accommodate the network of sprinkler systems siphoned increasing amounts of water from underground.

And there were consequences for our family. The growth brought new interest in hiking and mountain biking in the Pioneers, the same slopes our family had used to graze sheep for generations. Forest Service rangers scrutinized the grazing allotments of the few remaining sheep families to decide the best use of the land. Today they tell us the numbers are not in our favor. We wait as they grapple with these competing interests.

And downstream farm families, too, are anxious over the new uses of the river. They know the ravages of drought years and they know that a severe dry season will force the question—should the diminishing waters of the Big Wood be used for crops or golf courses? At the very least, several dry years will test the adage that in the West water does not flow downhill. It flows toward money.

A few years ago, a group of old-timers in the Wood River Valley took a close look at the community, as if for the first time, and decided to fight back. A crew from the highway department was ripping tall cottonwoods from the banks of the rechanneled Big Wood to straighten the parallel north-south road. Several angry residents chained themselves to trees. But it was too late. The river was irrevocably altered. A court order forced the protesters to unshackle themselves, and the cottonwoods were stripped away.

Now for some there seems little hope of slowing the rapid growth beyond some sort of natural disaster. And so each spring, with new snowmelt, the residents come out to watch the Big Wood rise, wondering if this will be the year the river rages out of control. It is not impossible, as my husband and I know. It happened on the Little Wood.

Old-timers who have lived in the Wood River Valley, for fifteen, twenty-five, fifty years or more, built homes years ago away from the river out of respect for its wildness. Today I've heard these same old-timers quietly cheering on the river each spring, as if a good flood would return the waters and the valley to familiar landscape.

"Go Big Wood, go," they whisper to each other, giving the thumbs-up sign, in the aisles of the grocery store, as they pass each other at the post office, at the video shop. It has become a kind of mantra, a secret society salute, code words to startle the memory and recall days when the Little Wood and the Big Wood rivers were not so far apart. "Go Big Wood, go," they repeat today, understanding there is little else left to say.

As for me, I retreat to the Little Wood, to our ranch, to days of hard work and quiet in this vast open space. I realize that our life along this river is a bittersweet experience threatened by perilous economic odds, capricious weather, and by our very proximity to the Big Wood. But perhaps each day is more valuable because of its vulnerability. And perhaps I can do little to save this place but walk the land, memorizing the moments of each day along my river.

Whitewater by Horse

John Rember

The chain hackamore is a cruel piece of machinery, consisting of a leather harness that goes around the head, short chains that attach to the harness, and a steel ring that the chains slide through. Resistance to being led causes the chains to bite deep into the nose and lip. The pain increases with the degree of resistance.

A chain hackamore breaks an animal to lead quickly, and when you've got a lot of animals in one string, having chain hackamores on everybody keeps everybody moving. Nobody can decide to sit down and bring the whole operation to a stop.

But the summer I was eighteen I used a chain hackamore for a far harsher purpose. I tied Festus, the giant mule entrusted to me by the U.S. Forest Service, to a tree and began beating him with a length of two-by-four. He'd back away, the rope would wind around the tree, the hackamore would tighten, and I'd hit him again. Within a few seconds, his head was flattened against the tree trunk, chains were winding into his lower lip, drawing blood, and his breath was coming in a hoarse scream of pain and terror. I bounced the two-by-four off his head and neck and shoulders until I couldn't lift it anymore.

When I was done, the only thing that kept Festus upright was the rope.

You might think that I felt shame at that moment, but I didn't. I thought I'd just killed Festus, and I was glad. Unfortunately, Festus was government property, a young, healthy, just-purchased mule, one of the biggest any of us at the Ranger Station had ever seen, able to pack an entire elk if he ever got packed down enough that he could be handled. I would be fired from my job as a Forest Service packer unless I could come up with an excuse for a dead mule covered with two-by-four marks. My career as a government employee would end when I showed up at the Seafoam Guard Station with one less mule than I had started with. I was also missing George, my saddle horse.

I should state right here that I did evil that day. You shouldn't torture helpless animals in chain hackamores. I have a minister friend, Enright, who went so far as to shoot a man who shot Henry, his horse. Enright was walking up to Henry, about to put his foot in the stirrup, when Henry fell over. When the hunter who had killed Henry came running up the hill, he found Enright with one foot on Henry's carcass.

"That's my elk," said the hunter. "Get your foot off it." Enright pointed to Henry's saddle. The guy started running down the hill, and Enright unholstered his .22 pistol and shot him in the ass.

Enright only had to do a little county jail time for this incident, because he drove his flesh-wounded victim to the emergency clinic in Stanley, lecturing him all the way about the evil that attends killing an innocent beast of burden. At the civil trial, Enright's attorney noted Enright's status as an emissary of God, quoted Walt Whitman and the Bible, and spoke at length on the suffering of dumb and loyal animals. The jury awarded the victim a dollar.

After Enright got out of jail he had a period of unemployment. He spent it hunting chukar partridge. After hunting chukars in the hills around the East Fork of the Salmon, chasing them up steep slopes only to have them vanish into rock piles and sagebrush, after missing them on the wing and then missing them on the ground, he told me that chukars were creatures of Satan. "The only way to hunt them is in the egg," he said.

Even Enright's concern for the weak and helpless had its flaws.

But not for nothing do we learn that most serial killers have a history of torturing frogs and kittens when they were children. Not for nothing do we shudder in the presence of men who break the noses and black the eyes of their wives, and in the presence of the wives who stay with them. Not for nothing do we turn our decent faces away from those who dance the weeping, bloody, ancient dance of the powerful and the powerless, and I remember that summer I was eighteen with a shudder, because nothing I will ever do will stop it from being the summer I tied an animal in a chain hackamore to a tree and beat him with a club.

Nothing will change the fact that Festus was a bad mule, either. When we had first put a packsaddle on him in the Forest Service corrals, he had broken a halter rope and bucked the saddle off inside of a minute. When we had tied him back up and cinched the saddle on him as tight as we could, we had only been able to pack him by throwing him down on one side, tying his kicking feet to the fence, and lashing a canvas-wrapped bale of hay to the top side of the saddle. Then we had to throw him down on the other side, lash another bale to the saddle, and finally let him up. Then we put a chain hackamore on him and trailed him ten miles behind a pickup, until he was dragging, bleeding from unshod feet, covered with foamy sweat and broken blisters, and the desperate wheeze of his breath could be heard in the pickup cab.

The irony of breaking a mule this way lay in the fact that I thought I was a good man with horses. I had watched my father break horses gently, working them with light hands, talking them into accepting the saddle and his presence on their back. When it came time to put a packsaddle on them, he had usually touched them and fed them and ridden them enough that they were curious rather than outraged when the straps were slipped down around their rumps and across their chests. I thought I could talk to horses that way. I thought they would understand me in the same way—that my father's ability to break horses was hereditary.

But I was working with two Forest Service foremen who prided themselves on being real cowboys, and even though I had been hired because I knew how to pack horses, it was clear that they didn't think much of my skill with mules. They knew how to break mules, they told me. They showed me their methods and at the end of a few weeks I was just as brutal to the animals as they were.

When they put me out on the Middle Fork of the Salmon with a string of fourteen mules, Festus was among them. I also was trailing two Percheron colts that were too young to work. People in the Forest Supervisors' offices in Challis and Boise would use the mules to pack in elk and deer that fall, and they wanted them packed down by the time hunting season rolled around. They wanted the Percherons gentle enough to pull the horse-drawn equipment in Forest Service pastures on the Middle Fork of the Salmon.

My job was to supply trail crews in what is now the Frank Church Wilderness, mostly along the Middle Fork, from Dagger Falls to the mouth of Loon Creek. I packed chain saws, trail graders, tents, food, harnesses, bedrolls, culverts, treated timber, and a complete kitchen and table service for eight, in green and white Forest Service glass, on those mules. On the evenings when I wasn't near a corral, I would hobble them and run them up a tributary canyon, pitching my tent at its mouth. I would put bells on the lead mules, and I got so I would come instantly out of a deep sleep if I heard a bell come too close. This was because there had been times I had slept while they had filed down past my tent and onto the trail. Once, by the time I had caught up with them, they had gone fifteen miles in hobbles, back to the Thomas Creek, the last place they'd had good pasture. I had learned that a mule can go faster in hobbles than a man can go in cowboy boots.

The saddle horse they gave me was twenty-five years old. His name was George, and he was a slow gentle old swaybacked sorrel gelding with arthritis in his shoulders. Riding him downhill started him into a side-to-side dance that produced little forward movement, and I soon learned to dismount at the slightest decline.

But other than that, George was all the horse I wanted. Down below Thomas Creek, the rattlesnakes were thick, and the slope so steep on the high side of the trail that I could hear them—but not see them—buzzing in the rocks a foot or two from my thigh. George would hear them, step away from them, and keep us both from harm's way, never breaking stride.

In the mornings, when I would fill the grain bucket, George would be waiting outside my tent. His teeth were getting short and he was losing weight. I'd give him more than his share of grain, put a halter on him, swing up on his bare back, and go get the mules.

Atop George, I was able to see a world marked by brittle sage and broken rock, by high summits still covered with June snow, by dry thunderclouds and the high dark shapes of hawks. And that was just on the rattlesnake side of the trail. On the river side, there was the flash of falling water, the white sand of riverside beaches, and the occasional drifting boats of the Middle Fork rafters.

It occurred to me, when I saw them, that the rafters were better off than me. After all, I had to work all day with half-wild mules and all they had to do was drink beer and watch the world float by. But there were times when I rode along stretches of rapids so rough that boats had been known to turn somersaults down them. Then—even if I was working the mules around a sharp cliffside corner a hundred feet above the water—I tended toward smug self-congratulation. A careful old horse can inspire smugness, even love, when your ears are ringing with the roar of whirlpools and the screams of people suddenly convinced they should have vacationed at a shuffleboard park.

I began to think that George and I could read each other's thoughts. I also began to think that he was getting thinner and thinner and before the summer was over, if I kept riding him ten or fifteen miles a day, he'd probably be ready for the knacker.

By July, no lives had been lost in the waterfalls of the Middle Fork. And nights, when I had hobbled the mules and had eaten my dinner of canned Spam and macaroni and cheese, I walked to where I could see campfires down on the sandbars. I heard guitars and laughter, and smelled sirloin.

I was a happiness voyeur. More than that I was a person astonished that two worlds could touch and yet remain separate. Twenty feet from where salmon sped upstream under the drifting boats, riverbank ferns gave way to grass and the occasional grazing deer, and twenty feet from that grew the stunted thick leaves of desert plants. Out on the water the sun warmed, but on the trail it dried and it burned.

A week before the day I tied Festus to the tree I had put the mules up a tributary canyon. In the morning when I went out to catch them, George wasn't waiting outside my tent. After I had the mules tied up, I tracked George's big hoofprints on up the canyon until, a couple of hours later, I reached the summit. George was there, and he looked up at me from the tiny meadow of short grass he was standing in.

"George," I said, and waved his halter at him. He stood still. I didn't have grain with me, but he'd never been hard to catch before. He looked at me sadly and turned his skinny rump to me and walked away, into the next drainage.

"George!" I yelled. But he was beyond hearing me. I could have caught him. Even in cowboy boots I could outrun him. But I was thinking he was going off to die. I thought there would be some good in letting him go. I thought maybe I could talk one of the Percherons into letting me put a saddle on him.

I walked back down to camp and began packing up. The experiment with the Percheron lasted somewhat less than eight seconds, but would have been entertainment if anybody other than the mules had been there to see it. I ended up riding a short mule named Johnny, and the dust beneath his hooves was deep and fine that week. Johnny didn't avoid the rattlesnakes, which now buzzed within striking distance of my neck.

In the evenings, after I had unpacked and tied the lead mules to trees, I would search for George in the high desert mountains above the river. There, I found old mines, a ruined fire lookout, small hillside springs that nourished, with tiny amounts of water, the wild orchards of abandoned homesteads. I found a rotting trapper's cabin at the intersection of two overgrown trails, with rusty traps still hanging on an inside wall. I found trees that had grown around horseshoes hung on their branches, caves littered with deer bones, and ancient ridge-top forests, twisted and small and wind-whipped. The sunsets that summer were fiery, and the water, looking like molten lead in the bottom of the canyon, reflected red light onto dusk-gray hillsides. When I had finished hunting George for an evening, I would walk down into darkness, put the bells on the lead mules, and go to bed.

The day I tied Festus to the tree had begun, for me, at daylight, and it had taken me until two in the afternoon to get the mules saddled and packed. I was heading from Indian Creek to Thomas Creek, a distance that would allow me to trail down the river, unpack, and settle in by dark.

But I made a mistake. I packed the kitchen on Festus. I suppose I did it to be able to brag about it later—I was going to tell the two cowboys from Challis that I had packed the kitchen boxes on the same mule we'd had to throw down to pack.

Festus had been a decent mule for a while. He was so tall I had had to pack him standing on a rock or a stump, but other than that he had been little trouble. He led well—the chain hackamore had done its work on his tender lower lip—and he hadn't bucked anything off for a week. I had usually packed the trail grader and plow and singletree and chains on him, which all together weighed a couple of hundred pounds and couldn't be damaged by anything short of a cutting torch.

But just as I was tying him into the string, Festus began bucking. He broke the cord that attached him to the next mule. He bucked his way out into a clearing, and then he began bucking in earnest. The plates and cups and bottles inside the kitchen boxes started clanging and tinkling, and first one box, and then the other, arced out and away from his saddle and crashed onto the ground. Then Festus got the saddle twisted down under him and went into a frenzy of kicking, twisting, and crow-hopping, breaking straps and dragging the saddle through the rocks until finally the last pieces of it fell off him.

I walked toward him slowly. In the softest of voices, I told him it was all right. Putting the kitchen on him was my mistake. As soon as I picked everything up, I'd pack him up again with the grader and plow, and we'd get on the trail. He let me put a rope through the ring in his hackamore, and I led him to a tree and tied him to it.

But as I left him and walked back to the pieces of saddle that littered the clearing, he kicked me. His foot caught me hard in my upper thigh.

I came off the ground long enough to realize I was flying. Then I hit and rolled. Then I lay there, thinking that my femur was broken and that I was going to die—because a broken femur will lose enough blood into the thigh muscle that you can bleed to death without even a break in the skin—and I was alone, and pretty soon the flies would be feasting on me, and the only time I'd ever float the Middle Fork would be when they floated my body out, and I wouldn't get to enjoy it because I would be dead. Festus had remembered that day when he'd first been made into a pack animal, and had bided his time, waiting for the perfect opportunity, and now had his revenge.

I wasn't nearly as patient as he had been. I crawled over to a camp table and pulled a two-by-four brace out from under it. I used it as a crutch to get to my feet, and limped and hobbled toward Festus.

By the time I was done my leg still hurt but I was feeling a lot better. I took the rope off Festus's hackamore and untied it from the tree. He fell over on his side and was still.

I packed the kitchen on another mule, and put a canvas around Festus's torn-up saddle and packed it on top of the kitchen, and finished tying the string together. When I was done I saddled Johnny and away we went. Five miles later I decided that I should have towed Festus to the Middle Fork and claim that he fell in and drowned, but then I decided I had had enough of mules, and of being the only human being in camp, and of the Middle Fork, and of the Forest Service. If they wouldn't fire me, I'd quit.

At Thomas Creek the next morning, I got out of my tent, stood up and found myself face-to-face with Festus. He had followed us downriver—at a distance—and although he looked terrible, he looked like he might live. I put George's halter on him and put him at the end of the string, without a packsaddle, and led him for a couple of days. Then, only partly because I was getting tired of the dust that rose up around Johnny's shoulders and swirled into my face, I put my riding saddle on Festus, put my foot in the stirrup, and swung up on top of him. I expected to die then and there.

A mule will always ride smoother than a horse, and Festus was smooth-riding for a mule. He was surefooted, and though he didn't avoid the rattlesnakes, he was enough taller than George that they would have had to stretch to get to me. For a week I waited for him to turn on me and buck me into a nest of snakes or wait until I wasn't watching and then kick me to the top of the nearest ponderosa. But he never did. He understood the reins and he wasn't in the least bit hard-mouthed. I began to think Festus and I could read each other's thoughts.

It was still July when I reached Rapid River, one of the main tributaries of the Upper Middle Fork, and camped with the trail crew that was working there. There, in the middle of the week, the news came over the Forest Service radio that we had an unexpected day off. I left my animals with the trail crew. They

promised not to lose any of them. They also said if George
showed up they'd put him in the corral.

On foot, I climbed up out of Rapid River, climbed against the
clock, climbed four thousand vertical feet, and climbed finally up
the steps of the farthest-from-civilization fire lookout of them all,
Little Soldier. Its lonely occupant welcomed me in, shook my
hand, and made me tea. Then, while he scanned a ragged horizon
for signs of burning forest, and I scanned it for signs of George, he
turned on his battery-powered radio and we listened in awe on the
day men first talked from the moon.

It was winter before George turned up in Challis. The Forest
Service put him out to pasture, and he lived another decade,
giving rides to Forest Service children and eating rolled oats. I was
congratulated by the cowboys for what I had done with Festus—
he packed out two elk that hunting season, although I thought for
a long time that he was just waiting for the right moment, and
then he was going to kill a human being, any human being, but
preferably me. The next summer I got a different job, as a
wilderness ranger in the Sawtooths. I was on foot, carrying a
backpack, and in the nearly thirty years between the time I took
the club to Festus and now, I can count on my fingers the times
I've been in a saddle. But I've never lost my temper at an animal
since that day.

Since that summer, I've read Walt Whitman, and I have come to
love that thirty-second poem of his *Song of Myself* that says he
could turn and live with the animals, because

> They do not sweat and whine about their condition,
> They do not lie awake in the dark and weep for their sins,
> They do not make me sick discussing their duty to God,
> Not one is dissatisfied, not one is demented with the mania
>   of owning things,
> Not one kneels to another, nor to his kind that lived thousands
>   of years ago,
> Not one is respectable or unhappy over the whole earth.

Without ever knowing the story of my encounter with Festus, my minister friend Enright has told me that he has come to believe that animals are morally superior to human beings, especially human beings like him and me. And although he dearly loves to hunt, he has finally given up hunting.

"Life is a spiritual journey," he tells me. "Live long enough, and you'll give up killing your fellow creatures. You have my word on it."

"What about chukars?"

"The chukar partridge is a creature of God when you're not chukar hunting," he says.

It's no use talking to him about it. He has sold his guns—one of them, the .22 pistol he sold to me.

"Don't shoot anybody with it," he told me, handing it my way. "Unless they shoot your horse."

Lately, Enright has become enamored of the story of Jonah. He preaches on it all the time, and his congregation has become sick of hearing how Jonah, disobeying God's call, booked a vacation cruise, became the worst kind of bad luck for the boat he was on, got thrown overboard, got eaten by a whale, and was regurgitated, not much worse for wear, at the place he had been told to go in the first place.

"The story of Jonah," he says, "proves that God has us all in a chain hackamore."

I tell him the story of Jonah was a good-enough metaphor in the first place and he doesn't need to mix it with another. But he does have a point. If life really is a spiritual journey, it's probably a lot like Jonah's cruise. Things happen to us even after we've refused them. Deep internal imperatives take us in directions we would never choose, and maybe those deep internal imperatives are just another way of saying *God*. Enright, who loves to hunt, finds himself unable to reconcile hunting with the killing of animals. Who or what told him to become the nonhunter he had become? Who told him to turn and live with the animals?

And yet I have learned that it isn't that easy. You can't just turn and live with them because you want to. Their world and ours, though close, do not often touch, and it's seldom they are bridged by anything other than violence. I would never tell Enright that to really know a chukar you have to shoot and eat it, and to really share thoughts with a mule you have to beat on him with a two-by-four, but at some level my experience has taught me these things, and at some level I resist taking the next step on my spiritual journey, because at some level I'm not sure who's got me by the nose.

From Salmon to Snake:
A River Addendum

William Studebaker

I grew up catering to the emotions of creeks and rivers: the North Fork of the Salmon, the Lemhi River, Yellow Jacket Creek, Camas Creek (just a few yards up from its confluence with the Middle Fork of the Salmon), and the Main Salmon. I have responded to highs and lows.

I learned to hold my breath in icy Yellow Jacket Creek, to swim at the bottom of an Idaho Power diversion-dam spillway on the Lemhi. When I was ten, my dad wrapped bicycle tubes around my chest and taught me to bodysurf on the Main Salmon River. And one summer, during a family vacation at Swan Lake in western Montana, I paddled a flatwater aluminum canoe. It belonged to Walt Blackadar and he instructed his daughter Ruth and me by demonstration and by fright. What he failed to show us, he taught by accident—accidents he created. His approach was direct.

Along about that time, Dad started building canoes. River canoes. I paddled...some. I rafted...some. I jet boated with Don Smith. I sat in my first kayak at Blackadar's up on the Bar Hill in Salmon.

Thirty years passed and I was at Tom and Farla Schiermeier's cabin near Stanley, Idaho, when the decade-long drought ended (1983–1993). I felt whimsical like an animal sniffing familiar water. I started shopping for a kayak. I bought a Dancer and taught myself to roll—something that hadn't been demonstrated thirty years before.

My neighbor Chris Huddleston and I hit moving water together. The moving water was a fright. Every ripple was an accident. But I'd learned from accident before, so I paddled with unanchored enthusiasm. I took my whitewater direct.

For several years now, I have paddled two or three times a week— at least two or three times every month of the year. Every member of my family—Judy, Tona, Rob, Tyler and Eric—has learned to paddle—some to be with me, some to lead me.

⌒⌒⌒

When I was young, I not only catered to creeks and rivers, I fantasized about water. My childhood fantasy was simple. I wanted to be the Salmon River. I wanted to be rain and snow and pour myself over some ground, enough to flow and to continue flowing. Flake to drop, drops to drip, drips to stream, streams to rivulet, rivulets to cataract, cataracts to cascade, cascades to creek, creeks to river, rivers to river—the Salmon River. And to do it all over again!

I would be the dripping of a glacier's foot or the rising of a spring that is the headwater. I would have moods and seasons. When the temperatures were right, I would grace the gills of sturgeon, drift food over mussels, give up my grip on silt sinking out of sight, clearing clear to the bottom. I would cuddle eel and fish, stroke every swimmer, and wear the rock that is the island of my other life. Everything in the end becoming river.

When the temperatures were right, I would lump up and slush out on low land. I would flood over myself, humping up shards of ice, grinding gravel, slicing trees. I would find faults, warm with the wind, crack my icy shelves like a rifle, chap the lips of creeks' mouths as they pressed against me. I would break banks, bend gravel bars, crush riprap, pushing everything to high ground. I would repent and pour myself over some earth, enough to flow and to continue flowing, and I would raise myself to be the man that is the boy.

I never dreamed less, saw no separation for me from the river that defined where I lived and how I traveled. Upriver was down (south); down was up (north). *Salmon* was the town, *the* Salmon was the river, *salmon* were fish, and like the fish I knew the Salmon was the River of No Return. But not in my wildest dream did I imagine the Salmon at Salmon would be salmonless. My fantasy was not prophetic or ecological, just a child's vision of the water.

For years I set my play by the rhythms of the Salmon, and when I was not on its shores, I was on a tributary: the North Fork, the Lemhi, Yellow Jacket Creek, Camas Creek, the Middle Fork, Panther Creek, Carmen Creek. All my childhood near water—I took it for granted and I studied it and its ways. The ways of the river became my secret religion, my secret Chuang Tzu, my secret...me.

Time like driftwood floated by and piled up a little farther on, then floated by and piled up a little farther on. I went on, too— studying, working, raising a family, building a house, micromanaging money. But now I have returned to my old ways. I have come to be a river. I have taken up kayaking and reprecipitated my faith.

I still love the Salmon River, the River of No Return, that hefts such wild loads as the Sawtooth National Recreation Area, the Frank Church Wilderness, and the longest free-flowing water course in the contiguous forty-eight states. I still dream its dream. I still know it better than any piece of water on earth. I have drunk from it, floated it, paddled it, fished it, swum it. I have lain in it to avoid the swelter of 103 degrees. I have ice-skated along its banks.

But now I live on the cliff above Rock Creek, a tributary to the Middle Snake, and it's the Snake I am becoming. In a small stretch called the Murtaugh, I have found myself again—that man who is boy.

The Murtaugh Stretch is the last free-flowing section of river on the Middle Snake. It runs for about fourteen miles between Milner Dam and Twin Falls falls. There are no bridges, no roads, no pipelines, no trails, no campgrounds, no motorized vehicles. It is wild and crazed water. By boaters' standards it is Class IV and V. Big water. Like the boy I was in Salmon some forty years ago, I go to the Murtaugh Stretch and I am thrilled by the movement, the shore lap of wave, the backrush of eddy, the wave walk. I listen to crash, slap, and pop of water piling and falling its way downstream, west, toward my house and family. That is how I get my dopamine: crash, slap, and pop.

Like a dyslexic kayaker I cannot always tell up from down, particularly when everything has gone over. However, I know that the Murtaugh Stretch of the Middle Snake River is not the Salmon River. The Salmon is undammed; it is free-flowing from head to mouth. But I have recycled my life and here I am, and the Murtaugh Stretch has become my fantasy. In it I dream of all rivers, of all water, of all becoming. It is my dragon.

When I say Murtaugh Stretch, I mean slap, drop, twist, spin in downstream foam. I mean hydraulic squirt. I mean rapids like Maybelline that will suck the paint off your boat and give you a chiropractic back pop, neck snap, and shoulder stretch. I mean rapids like Big Eddy, Misty, Junk Yard, Pair-a-Dice, and Let's Make a Deal. I mean a little free-flowing whitewater that's trying to be a river. That's worth every politician's skin. That's every person's child: free to be water, to pour over some ground, to find the best way down, even if that down is north, the way I was headed when I left Salmon down the Salmon and out of town scattering to somewhere to re-center my life.

Now I paddle almost every day. I am closer to being a river than I was when I sat on the banks of the Salmon and watched the waves and ripples as chinook rose, finning their way toward Stanley, toward death. Perhaps each was the last death. Perhaps as I am writing, the last chinook is dying for us all. I don't know. What I do know I learned from the rivers. There are no balances, only extremes. One extreme weighed against another does not balance. It alters the flow. Something gives, something is given. I have given up the Salmon for the Snake. I have my stretch of water. I have my fix. A single wave is worth a dozen reservoirs. One waterfall can fertilize ten thousand things.

I have placed my finger on the Snake River's pulse and I feel my own heart beating. We are good for now. We must get better. We must make an excess of ourselves, flooding the mind with free whitewater, and outpace those who would stop the flow.

I cannot be the Salmon. My life is reformed. I am becoming the Murtaugh Stretch of the Middle Snake River, paddling its life to save my own.

Paradise and Purgatory:
The Coeur d'Alene River

Julie Titone

It's a warm June afternoon, I'm driving beside the North Fork of the Coeur d'Alene River and am drowsy in a way no amount of coffee will cure. With no pressure to be anywhere soon, I park my Subaru atop a high riverbank, grab a fleece vest to use as a pillow, and look for a place to nap.

A water-carved rock calls out my name. It's the Barcalounger of boulders, shaped to cradle my body. I'm soon snuggled in, halfway between water and invisible road, lying lizardlike in the sun and out of the breeze. There's an emerald pool just beyond my feet. The current beyond makes a sweet swoosh that muffles the noise of the occasional passing vehicle. Those drivers, poor souls, don't know what they're missing.

⌒⌒⌒

The North Fork is one of Idaho's most accessible and pristine rivers. You aren't likely to find it written up in glossy tourism magazines, though. The rest of the Coeur d'Alene River system has been so desecrated that travel writers don't bother to look closely at the North Fork, which starts as a trickle up yonder between Lake Pend Oreille and Montana, then loops down toward Interstate 90.

The smaller South Fork also starts near Montana, near Lookout Pass, and parallels the interstate highway. It's a sad relic of a river, contaminated with metals from a century of mining operations. It meets the North Fork near Enaville, where the landscape flattens and the toxic metals settle on the riverbanks and bed.

Given this scenario, you'd think a water lover would lavish her time and thoughts only on the beloved North Fork. But at the beginning of a new century, there's trouble in paradise, and hope in the purgatory that industry created during the dozen decades past.

I look at the river through the eyes of two people. One of them knows the river as a canoeist, a fly-fisher, a camper, a napper. The other person, the journalist, is paid to learn about the Coeur d'Alene. I've sat in many meetings, watching well-intentioned people butt heads, and scratch heads, as they debate how to deal with the metals pollution. I've watched a dying swan, rendered helpless by the lead it has swallowed, stagger and flap in a channel off the lower river.

I've journeyed a mile underground into the Lucky Friday mine, fascinated by the other-worldliness of the lighted tunnels where hot water seeps in dark corners. I expected to meet Yoda around each bend, but instead met men who work far harder for their paychecks than I ever will. They smiled at this smudged woman in their midst, showed me how to use their drills. One man confided that he couldn't imagine any other way to make a living.

The Coeur d'Alene River is about jobs, journeys, simple pleasures and complex decisions. Here's some of what I've learned about it.

⌐⌐⌐

Jo Babin points to a rock that kids use as a diving pad for plunging into the North Fork. She recalls for me how, as a young mother in Spokane, the wildness of city life got her fretting about its impact on her kids. So she told her husband: "I'm taking them to the river for the summers."

*She did. They lived in a tent on land the family had near Prichard.
When the kids ran wild in the woods, played in that clear water, she
didn't worry.*

*Now, in her grandmother years, Jo's favorite hot-summer-day pastime
is to put her custom "Cadillac" inner tube in the river and laze her way
downstream. She tells me she thinks those canoeists who go out in the
high, cold spring runoff are crazy. I laugh, and tell her I'm one of
them.*

*What fun. Put on your wet suit, strap on a helmet if the river's really
hauling ass, and careen around those cliffs, navigate around the fallen
trees. Bounce through the rapids. Yee-haw.*

᙭᙭᙭

For most of its seventy miles, the North Fork of the Coeur d'Alene
is flanked by conifers. It grows steadily, fed by streams that race
headlong through mountain ravines. You can paddle past cliffs of
green and granite here; tease a trout; savor the slow sweep of a
bald eagle's wings.

So why does Joe Peak say, "I lay awake at night worrying about the
river"?

First, you should know that Joe owns the Enaville Resort, a restaurant
that sits beside the North Fork about a mile from Interstate 90.
It's a tall log building with family quarters upstairs and decor
that's half thrift store, half lodge. Locals call it the Snakepit. They
can count on Joe for sloppy-juicy North Fork Burgers and for
opinions about anything that's happening in the Silver Valley.

At spring runoff, kayakers stop by for burgers and pitchers of
Moose Drool. Fall is prime time for fly-fisher folk to visit, pausing
briefly in their pursuit of gullible cutthroat.

Fishing's not as good as it used to be though, not by a long shot.
Flooding is on the rise. And as if those worries aren't enough for

Joe, there's the fear that the river will become polluted, its shoreline abused by the fast-growing number of visitors from the fast-growing cities to the west.

The North Fork's possible futures are so alarming that they're turning some local business people into agitators. Joe and his neighbors upriver are nagging the politicians for new laws and enforcement of existing ones: zoning laws, water-protection rules. Whatever it takes to keep the river pretty and clean.

They want action.

"This needs to be in place as of yesterday," bed-and-breakfast owner Claudia Childress wrote to county commissioners. She was asking for installation of a sewage dump station that would make it easier for trailer owners to keep waste out of the river. She's not one to mince words. Nor is Dick Rifkind, who owns a tree nursery and 365 acres along the river. He feels so strongly about protecting the North Fork that his fellow county planning commissioners threatened to oust him from a meeting for angrily arguing against allowing a recreational subdivision in the floodplain.

"The North Fork is a magnificent river," he says. "If Shoshone County is going to prosper, we have to do everything we can to take care of it."

Dick doesn't plan to develop his waterfront, but thinks an upscale resort somewhere on the river could help the economy. It would hardly fit in with the traditional use of the seventy-mile North Fork, though.

This is a blue-collar playground. When Silver Valley residents haven't been logging the slopes above it or dredging for gold in its feeder streams, they've been hunting, camping, and fishing here. For decades, that meant piling into cars and heading up dirt roads.

"Everybody was in a sedan. We took a Hudson, Oldsmobile, or Buick," recalls Wallace native John Sprecht, who works for the

Forest Service. "Now, you have four-wheel-drives, Jeeps, pickups, ATVs, motorcycles."

⌐⌐⌐

A helicopter is a great way to get deep into the Coeur d'Alene country, providing you're prepared for the sights you're going to see.

On this day, photographer Chris Anderson and I head into the air with a biologist who is studying the elk population east of the North Fork. He's going to radio-collar some elk, but first must dart them with a tranquilizer gun. From the air. That requires dicey flying, so the pilot wants his passengers temporarily out of the chopper and out of danger. He sets us down on a mountain top.

At first, Chris and I joke about what we'll do if the pilot doesn't come back. We take inventory of our survival gear, which amounts to one Swiss Army knife and six cookies. After that, there's little to do but relax and take in the 360-degree view of the national forest. A sad reality settles in. The face of each mountain, ridge after ragged ridge, is scratched with logging roads and shaved haphazardly with clear-cuts.

When the helicopter returns, I am uneasy about heading back home. To a house made of wood.

⌐⌐⌐

In the 1970s, the Coeur d'Alene River Road was paved and the Forest Service put campgrounds higher up the drainage. Campers now come in record numbers from Coeur d'Alene, Post Falls, Spokane. Hunting season lures people from around the country. From the perspective of local folks, the best of the visitors leave money at the restaurants and bars. They attend church retreats at the old Shoshone work camp, buy gas at the new Texaco.

The worst of them leave litter. It's not uncommon to see beer cans floating in the water, toilet paper behind bushes.

And while better roads have brought more people, there are fewer fish for them to catch. The bull trout are long gone. Cutthroat still hang out in the upper, catch-and-release stretch. But, as logger Bill Hagameier laments, "They're just not there any more, the real big ones."

Biologists attribute the decreasing fish population to a shortage of pools, where trout like to lurk. The pools have filled up. Nearly everyone blames that on clear-cutting and logging roads that allow water to run off the mountainsides too quickly, sending rocks tumbling into the river. Logging continues, though on a smaller scale; the Forest Service says it needs money from timber sales to pay for landscape repairs.

"The North Fork used to be a deep, narrow river. Now, after July, the water is so low it's very difficult to float," says riverside resident Jack King. He thinks the quick way to improve fishing is to scrape some rocks out of the North Fork. Forest Service biologist Ed Lider shakes his head at that idea. "We could invest millions of dollars dredging the Coeur d'Alene River, and I think the first flood would fill it up," Lider says.

Ed is hopeful that, in the long run, the river will heal. He's encouraged that recent floods have caused homes to be moved from the floodplain. Now, the river can be free to re-create itself.

⌒⌒⌒

I'm witness to a flood and, for a few moments, have stopped thinking about the human trauma it is causing.

It's simply overwhelming, this sight of Mother Nature taking control, filling the river until it nearly reaches the deck of the Cataldo Bridge, carrying trees and tires and anything else it can grab. Water laps at the freeway. Pine Creek, normally a trickle, has become an "outta-my-way" torrent. The air is electrified, the winter sky blinding blue. I am enthralled.

めめめ

Floods and so-so fishing aren't enough to keep people away from the North Fork. Because the floodplain ordinance and septic rules limit construction of homes and cabins, recreational vehicles have become the summer abode of choice on the private lands that extend from I-90 to the national forest fourteen miles upriver.

Grace Myers and her late husband sold much of their riverside farmland for use as a recreational subdivision. "Why should two people sit on all that land when other people could enjoy it?" Still, she remembers fondly the wilderness she first saw up the North Fork in 1948.

Grace has retired in Coeur d'Alene. Like many who remain here, she misses the uncluttered hayfields that served as a foreground for mountain vistas. She and others fear water pollution from people who don't use outhouses; who throw dishwater on the ground. They have lots of recommendations for dealing with these problems, including new rules and education programs. A 1983 river master plan contained similar ideas; it got shelved by the county. Nobody is quite sure why. Now the North Fork folk are blowing the dust off it, trying again.

めめめ

Dump, scoop, tamp the dirt down. Scoot some rocks along the edge. Voila! A streambed!

I'm in Government Gulch on a hot summer day, watching a giant excavator do its thing above the South Fork of the Coeur d'Alene. Operator Beth Latina is like a kid in a sandbox, working/playing in this brown sweep of land that was one of the most polluted spots on the Bunker Hill industrial complex. It's where the zinc smelter—squatting right down over Government Creek—spewed the worst kind of acid rain, further denuding the logged-over hillsides. The buildings are gone, mostly. The creek has been rerouted while the land is scraped clean of metals-polluted soil.

With a delicate twist of the excavator's gargantuan claw, the land changes contour and Government Creek flows from a diversion ditch into its sinuous new path. I find it pleasantly ironic that a woman is in control of the machine that has given birth, or rebirth, to a mountain stream.

☙☙☙

It's been called Lead Creek and much worse. But the South Fork of the Coeur d'Alene may deserve a new name: Resurrection River.

After suffering decades of the worst kind of mining pollution, cleanup efforts are making a difference. Zinc suspended in the water still keeps most fish away, but the South Fork often glints like crystal. While most of its shoreline is anything but natural, efforts are underway to return vegetation to some of it.

Communities that turned their backs on the South Fork decades ago are taking another look.

"It's actually a great benefit," says Kellogg city planner Walter Hadley, who is working to develop a riverside greenbelt through his hometown. Park benches, trees, and a paved trail now top the Kellogg levees that could become part of a proposed seventy-two-mile hiking and biking trail along the abandoned Union Pacific railroad tracks that parallel the river.

People were long warned to stay away from the South Fork. Being invited to stroll along its banks is a remarkable turn of events, given its one hundred-year status as one of the country's most contaminated rivers.

"People are even catching fish in the South Fork, up by Big Creek," says Silver Valley old-timer John Yergler. "I wouldn't eat 'em, but some people are catching them."

There's still so much zinc in the South Fork that a lot of fish never venture into it, veering instead into the North Fork. Some Lake Coeur d'Alene cutthroat do run up to the clean headwaters of the

South Fork to spawn; I envision them holding their fishy noses as they scurry past the former smelter site, which still leaks metals from a huge tailings impoundment.

⌒⌒⌒

In the mountains beyond the town of Mullan and the uppermost mine, I follow Stefan Wodzicki, a newly minted scientist, through the forest tangle. Ferns brush his long legs and my short ones; prickly devil's club snags us. We're headed toward the top stretch of the South Fork, which is what the entire river used to be: full of insects, shaded, burbling over smooth rocks colored rose and aquamarine. Stopping to squat beside a massive root wad, the corpse of a cedar upended ages ago, I stare into the stream until I'm embarrassed by my absence from the human who brought me here. Instead of interviewing him, I am listening to the water. The water has so much to say.

⌒⌒⌒

Before white settlement, the South Fork was a fish-filled torrent that poured into a lowland Shangri-La. After arriving in 1884, pioneer W.R. Wallace reported catching 247 trout in one day on Placer Creek.

The city that bears Wallace's name was first known as Cedar Swamp. Cedars still scrape the sky above the South Fork's headwaters. Downstream, the only hint of the historical swamps are ancient stumps that punctuate a lagoon near Smelterville.

It's impossible to envision the South Fork's future without understanding its past. By the 1880s, mines were dumping waste rock directly into its feeder streams. Much of it was a tan, powdery residue left from the early crude process of separating valuable ore from worthless rock.

Sometimes the miners built dams to hold back the waste rock, but spring floodwaters always won out. The earthen barriers burst, carrying zinc, lead, arsenic, and cadmium toward Lake Coeur d'Alene, the Spokane River, and beyond.

Along the way, the heavy metals killed fish, wildlife, livestock, pets and vegetation. Mining camps such as Wallace and Kellogg sprung up, and human waste was added to the foamy current. The South Fork stank. Meanwhile, much of the shoreline was replaced by dikes to protect the towns from flooding. Construction of Interstate 90 in the 1960s shoved the river around until it was little more than water in a ditch. It was 1968 before all the mines used settling ponds to limit contamination, despite expert advice to do so that dated back to 1933. In 1972, riverside communities approved a construction bond aimed at keeping raw sewage out of the water.

With the 1980s came a big drop in silver prices, leading to the closure of many mines and the Bunker Hill smelting complex. The federal cleanup of the twenty-one-square-mile Bunker Hill Superfund site is nearly complete, but a lot of remediation remains to be done along the South Fork. That includes getting shrubs and trees to take root.

"You have to have vegetation to have bugs, and you have to have bugs to have fish," says Marti Calabretta. She's in charge of state cleanup projects done cooperatively with the mining companies. Most of that effort has been to pull toxic mine tailings away from the most polluted tributaries, with the goal of keeping zinc out of the river and getting fish back into it.

That's not good enough for some valley residents. "What good does it do to have fish coming up the South Fork when children don't have a good place to go fishing?" asks Sandi Lockhart of Osburn.

Ron Garitone grew up fishing the river in its clean stretch, upstream of Mullan. Now he's retired, the mayor of Wallace and gung ho to beautify the riverbank that greets visitors to the Shoshone County seat—even though it is overshadowed by the interstate highway. Whitewater-crazy boaters aren't waiting for the beautification project. They come to Wallace each spring to surf springtime waves that rage through the channelized river. There's been talk of designating a kayaking park between Wallace and Kellogg, enhanced by strategically placed boulders.

The South Fork isn't deep enough for powerboats, and most of it is too noisy with freeway sounds to be pleasant for paddlers. If Kellogg's planner can find a way to build a launch site in the corridor of rock levees, he'd like to see canoes set off from his town and float toward the quiet, isolated stretch of river between Pinehurst and Enaville.

Marti says folks in her town of Osburn enjoy tossing rafts in the gravelly South Fork and floating a couple of miles. "When I think of the future, twenty years from now, I think my grandkids will be on the beach, swimming," she says. "And, hopefully, fishing."

⌒⌒⌒

I tell people I'm going to canoe the South Fork, just to get their reactions. Which is always: The freeway river? It's shallow, it's ugly. Why would anybody want to do that?

Because I want to write about the river and it would help to see it from the water, I reply. Mostly, though, it's because I've never done it before. And avid paddlers collect rivers in the same way Audubon folks check birds off their life lists.

An equally water-crazy friend, Brian Burns, contributes his sturdy Coleman canoe to the adventure. We launch at Big Creek on a cool March day. The water is amazingly clear. Trucks roar by on the interstate, but we're too busy staying off gravel bars to notice. Brian and I find a surprise: a bona fide, Class III rapid at Elizabeth Park. It seems like a piece of the original river that refused to be ruined. We have lunch, portage the boat, and head through the depressing rock chute created by the levees at Kellogg. Next, at the former Bunker Hill site, big trucks carry off toxic sediments dug out of the Smelterville flats. When we finally leave the freeway at Pinehurst, where the pines truly begin, silence falls on us like a benediction. It's just a couple miles now to the confluence of the South and North Forks, and the start of the lower Coeur d'Alene River.

～～～

To many eyes, the lower Coeur d'Alene looks like paradise. A languid waterway fringed by trees. A place where osprey fly, boats buzz by. It's wide and calm. Much of it threads between the lateral lakes—Rose, Killarney, Blue, Black, Medimont—all of them retreats for fishermen, duck hunters, bird watchers.

"It's so beautiful that people don't realize it is kind of nasty," says Idaho Department of Parks and Recreation employee Leo Hennessy.

The nastiness is that chemist's brew of metals that lurk in the banks and bottom of the river. So far, cleanup of the mining wastes has focused on the South Fork on the theory that cleaning downstream would be fruitless unless upstream sources of metals are eliminated. Now, attention is turning to the lower river.

But what's to be done about the environmental hazard? Should the mine tailings be dug out, treated with chemicals, covered with rock or shrubs? Or simply ignored? Should low dams be built in the chain of lakes, raising the water level and keeping swans that feed there from ingesting leaded soil?

The answers to these questions will determine what the river's lower stretch looks like in coming decades. Attempts at restoration will cost millions and be debated in court.

There was no doubt in the mind of the late Henry SiJohn that the effort must be made. Henry was an elder of the Coeur d'Alene tribe, a retired teacher. His parents took him as a child to dig water potatoes in the river. The potatoes began to taste metallic. The family stopped going to the river.

"Fish and wildlife are given to mankind by the Creator for his survival," he would say. "What happens to the animals soon happens to man."

The thirty-three-mile lower river begins at Enaville. Much of its first six miles is surprisingly remote, separated by a ridge from the

noise of Interstate 90. You see mallards and mergansers there, and
kids swinging from ropes that dangle from bridges. You see the
reflection of cedars mirrored in deep waters.

The river loses speed as the landscape flattens. Rocks washed
down from the North Fork form shifting gravel bars. South Fork
floods bring reddish mine tailings that cover the riverbanks all the
way to Lake Coeur d'Alene.

The flat land below Old Mission State Park is nothing but tailings.
From 1933 to 1967, mine owners dredged sediment from the river
every winter to keep the channel open. Some 34.5 tons of metal-
laden dirt were spread over hundreds of acres, twenty feet deep.

If the metals stayed put, there would be less cause for concern. But
the shoreline erodes. Two big reasons for that become clear shortly
after the river flows under the I-90 bridge at Cataldo: powerboats
and the water level.

From early summer through late fall, the river rises along with
Lake Coeur d'Alene as the Post Falls Dam gates on the far side of
the lake are closed. Shoreline vegetation that could slow erosion
can't get established because of the fluctuations. When those
naked banks are exposed to boat wakes, lead washes into the river.

An estimated twelve thousand boat trips are made on the river
each year. Banning boats would be a cheap remedy to erosion. But
a politically impossible one, or so everyone says. The signs in no-
wake zones are frequently ignored.

Only two commercial farmers remain on the river. Frank Frutchey
and Mike Schlepp have spent years and "blood, sweat, and tears"
learning which fertilizers bind metals in the soil. They've learned
how to grow grass that is used not as feed, but for its seed.

The farmers' rock used to protect the riverbanks. That's being tried
as an experiment to keep the toxic soils from washing into the river;
the rock berms may keep some boaters from their favorite camping

and picnicking spots. But nothing will keep boaters off the river or away from the shore, much of which is theirs, collectively. It is part of the state's Coeur d'Alene River Wildlife Management Area.

The goal of environmental agencies will be to clean up the spots where people are exposed to the most metals. But if they fail to also keep metals out of the South Fork, each flood will bring a new layer of toxins to the Lower Coeur d'Alene.

Some people think cleanup money is wasted. They want Mother Nature to take her course, growing plants and clearing the riverbanks at her own speed.

"Sure, we have helped it out a little, but just look at that creek," says Lucia Anderson, who lives in the lakeside town of Harrison near the mouth of the river. "I mean, that river is taking care of itself."

Mike, whose fields are being gobbled up by the river, disagrees.

"The idea of letting anything happen naturally is late by about 100 years."

࿔࿔࿔

Sam Lombard doesn't need an advanced scientific degree to find evidence that Mother Nature is holding her own along the lower river. He has the sharp eyes of a seven-year-old. Time and again, he presents his mother and me with some natural treasure he's discovered on a beach or gravel bar. This time, his bright eyes peer from under an oversized ballcap at the amazing thing in his hand. It's a frog, breathing hard and seeming suspicious about its fate. Sam looks intrigued. And resigned. He knows he has to let the critter go.

It's time to get back in the canoe. The boy sits in the middle, trolling with his little fishing pole. The water parts in front of the bow, making that lovely V-shaped wake that I would follow anywhere. As I steer the boat I picture Sam with his brown hair gone gray, picture him coming back to the Coeur d'Alene River. And finding another frog.

What the River Says

"—that is what I say." —William Stafford

Robert Wrigley

If you were a salmon and had made your way for a couple of years in the Pacific, and had eluded predators and gillnets and passed by several thousand brightly colored lures and flies and baited hooks, and had managed, by dint of power and tirelessness, according to some spark of memory or instinct, to get up the ladders and around the nine dams on the Columbia and the Lower Snake, and past the last slackwater reservoir at Lewiston, Idaho, you might arrive here finally, where I am, at the bottom end of Hells Canyon, at the mouth of your namesake stream. You might be here, though few of your kind do make it this far, and most that do are hatchery fish, still rugged and strong, but spawned at fish factories like the ones at Rapid River, near Riggins, or farther upstream, across the state, at Stanley Basin.

If, on the other hand, you were a wild fish, you might exhibit something a little like relief here, a little like joy or even love; no one knows, you might actually sense the very pebbles you were born out of. You might hole up in these deep pools at the confluence of your river and the Snake; you might roll and bask, rest up for a while, luxuriate in the odd, primordial knowledge of your original water, then head off, upstream again, through the many rapids—Eye of the Needle, Snow Hole, China Elkhorn, Big Mallard, Salmon Falls—all the way to the river's headwaters at

Galena and up a side creek there, to a bed of sand and pea gravel, where you'd deposit your eggs in a redd you sculpted with your tail, or, if you were a male, where you'd spread your milt over that same redd, fertilizing the eggs of the mate whose laying you stood guard to, and who, like you, will soon be dead and fed on by a bear or a clutch of lucky ravens. By anyone's measure, your journey is heroic, difficult in times immemorial, before dams and fisheries, before sonar and monofilament and high-tech tackle, before dewatering from irrigation and runoff of herbicides and the noxious spill from feedlots and ranches raising cattle and sheep. Your scarcity in the river named for you is one of North America's greatest environmental shames. And the source of it all, this still beautiful river, clear and cold, a river made of many forks and tributary streams, what shall we call it when you are all gone, you survivors, you throwback anachronisms, you apparently doomed, romantic symbols of human folly and contempt? When that day comes, if it comes, the river will be a monument, a tombstone, a cenotaph, and what joy we take in its beauty, its rapids, its postcard scenery, will be tempered by the elegy of its name.

⌒⌒⌒

I have set foot in or floated over or looked upon many miles of the Salmon River and its tributaries. I have fished for trout on the East Fork of the South Fork and on the Secesh. I have picked perfect pie cherries at the old homestead near the Wind River pack bridge. I have camped at Bear Lake, in Cougar Basin, and known that the spill from the lake will eventually flow past this spot at the Salmon's mouth. I have hunted chukar on the breaks above Riggins and visited with Sylvan Hart, better known as Buckskin Billy, at Five Mile Bar on the Main, the actual "River of No Return."

But that part of the Salmon I know best, and, by my knowing, love most, is the fifty-two miles or so from where I am today— leaned against a rock hot from the sun, at the confluence with the Snake—upstream to White Bird Creek. The Lower Salmon, this stretch is called. It's the bottom of the whole, nowhere-dammed,

entirely free-flowing system. It can be reached by gravel road from
the Idaho side in three places—Hammer Creek, Graves Creek,
Eagle Creek—but the best way to see it, to know it, is by boat, a
float boat—raft, kayak, drift boat—*downstream,* the direction in
which it is first known by the salmon fry hatched along its reaches,
the way it is encoded in them: a source, somewhere to come home to.

I have learned, over the last decade or so, a few things about this
stretch of river: where the remnants of Chinese rock houses can
be found, primitive but sturdy shelters where former railroad
workers holed up away from the white-racist towns to mine a little
gold and get by; where Elmer and Eva Taylor ranched at Rice
Creek, across from American Bar; where the best white sand
beaches are for camping; where the cliff swallows sing and chitter
in Blue Canyon; where Jackson Sundown worked on a ranch near
Wapshilla Creek. Sundown was a Nez Perce Indian who escaped
to Canada from the battle of the Bear's Paw, in Montana, and
reappeared in Idaho a few years later, and who was a world
champion rodeo cowboy at age fifty-three, a genuine, larger-than-
life legend.

I've camped all in all a week of nights on the tiny beach just below
the Eye of the Needle, less than a mile from the Snake, and once
put my hand ever-so-lightly on a cold, sleepy Western diamondback
coiled among some bunchgrass there. It took me three hard prods
with a mullein stalk to get him to rattle and leave. I ruined my
right shoulder trying to throw a rock across the river at Billy Creek,
though on that last, painful attempt, I made it and thus feel no
need to try again. And once, flat-water complacent, thinking
myself still half a mile upstream, I blundered into the blind ess
curve of China Creek Rapid on the ugly wrong side, and nearly
made my desperate ferry across to the run on the left, only to
wind up with the raft in a hole so deep there was no horizon but a
round wall of froth. The boat inched its way up the hole's bottom,
outward edge, but when I cleared the oars it started slipping down
again. If we had gone all the way back, where the water piled over
the truck-sized boulder behind us, the force of that plummet-rush
on the stern would have flipped the raft like a hotcake; my wife

and I would have been in that hole underneath the raft then, in the blender swirl of the oars and the round-and-round churn of the water. But instead, I plunged the blades back in and we held there, until the edge of the overflow half-filled the raft, and three or four hundred gallons later—five seconds? seven?—we scowed out and washed away like a waterlogged stump.

One night on the beach at Smoky Hollow, I woke up stiff from sleeping on the sand. Sand is a good bed; it will accept your contours, you can burrow down in it and be supported all along your length. But it is hard. Your very weight compresses it eventually to the offspring and someday progenitor of stone. Anyway, I love sleeping on the beach, despite the occasional large but harmless sand spiders that scuttle over my face, because sleeping there is, in ways only those who frequent country truly empty of extensive human habitation can know, absolutely "under the stars." That night at Smoky Hollow, there was no wind when I woke, though the river's constant wash resembled a breeze through branches and needles. The riffle just downstream from where we camped splashed and plunged. I must have groaned when I rolled from my side onto my back, and that moan let my son know I was at least semiconscious. He was thirteen then, and he said, "Dad, look at the stars." I've never seen anything like the sky that night, before or since; not in the mountains, not in the desert, nowhere. It was close to three A.M.; I checked my watch to be sure. There were, of course, more stars than ever, but it wasn't just numbers that dazzled us so. It was as though the sky as we slept had come closer, had closed in on us like some gigantic and curious animal. It was all eyes and personality; it was intimate. I felt, we felt, as close to God as we would ever be. There was something enormous around and inside us, and to this day the only thing I can compare it to is love.

The river of my childhood was the Mississippi. By virtue of its immensity alone it was dangerous. This was near St. Louis; there were twenty-six locks and dams between us and the river's mouth at New Orleans. It was a river of commerce, plied north and south by a near constant convoy of tugs and barges. It was a river of historical and literary significance. By the time I was fifteen I'd read *The Adventures of Tom Sawyer*, and *Life On the Mississippi*, and finally, ultimately, *The Adventures of Huckleberry Finn*. I think I knew even then that the river was a mystical thing, what T.S. Eliot would describe as "a strong, brown God"; that, despite the dams and the commercial activity, the endless string of towns and cities along its banks, it was not then and never would be completely tamed. Though St. Louis and Rock Island and Memphis might pump their sewage into its flow, it was, underneath its mud and muck and sludge, the pure melt of snow from the upper Midwest and from the eastern slope of the Rockies. If it had not yet prevailed, it could and someday it would. But one thought twice about eating fish from its waters; one was understandably reluctant about getting in.

My introduction to western rivers came early in my childhood. I remember, during a family vacation in the fifties, sitting on the rocky bank of the Big Thompson River, below Estes Park, Colorado, and thinking I'd never seen water so clear and elemental, thinking as well that it was a wishful, unreasonably hyperbolic name. There was nothing "big" about it. I remember on another trip, high on a rock overlooking the upper Rio Grande, in southern Colorado, being stunned by the view: this pearly flow, supplemented there and there and there again by other equally perfect streams, all down a green and forested valley, as far as my eye could see. And in my early twenties, having moved to Montana to study writing, I learned that I could watch such rivers, and fish in them, and immerse myself in their icy flows, far longer and far more regularly than I could read anybody's poems.

Because I was a lover of maps, I studied mine and came very close to memorizing western Montana: the Clark Fork, the Bitterroot, the forks of the Flathead, the Kootenai, the Yaak. The Mississippi of my childhood had its tributaries, too. The Missouri itself, from its headwaters just over the Continental Divide in Montana, entered the Big River barely twenty miles from my home; the

Ohio came in a hundred miles south. But every school kid thrashing his way through a social studies or geography lesson knew that. What other waters were there? Why could I not say then—why can I not say today—where the Meramac joins the Mississippi?—where the Illinois?—where the Des Peres?

This is not easy for me to understand, but I think I have to say that I came of age looking at western rivers, that the western landscape, vast as it was, became something I could actually see. Among the grand flatnesses of midwestern prairies, I think I could not understand drainages, watersheds, the way it all connected, a vast woven fabric of land and descent. Maybe the true nature of gravity eluded me there, as one who has not fallen can never see it as the verity it is.

And I thought, when I moved to Idaho in 1977, that it would be like western Montana all over again: mountains and rivers, mountains and rivers, if not without end then beyond anyone's ability to number. But I was wrong. Despite its plenitude of mountains, Idaho is far more a state of rivers than Montana is, which is to say, it is a geography, dominated not by massive ranges and broad valleys, but by its rivers and their canyons: the long hook of the Snake, from its Yellowstone headwaters and its curl south and west across the southern part of the state, to its hard, westward turn into Washington at Lewiston, may be the most formidable. The Snake is, however, to its glory and misfortune, Idaho's Mississippi. For me, it is the Salmon, the entire system of it within the confines of this one state that has been my home for most of my adult life, that signifies, that characterizes, that sums up the place.

Much of this significance comes from the fact that the river is free-flowing, but there is also the character of the land it drains: most of the largest remaining expanse of undeveloped land— wilderness, we call it—in the lower forty-eight. There is no other river like this one anywhere in the nation, outside of Alaska, and for this reason it seems to me that the Salmon is not simply the soul, the heart, the truest, purest bloodline of the state lucky enough to contain it; it is the remnant soul of the nation itself, a country so blessed by rivers that we must have thought, we European makers of civilizations, that they would never end and, thus, by our ignorance or enthusiasm, our greed or desperation, we proceeded to inflict ourselves and our damages on them all, even this one, one of our last, and truly one of our holiest.

⌐⌐⌐

For me, the Salmon River was, in the beginning, like most western rivers I have known, not much more than scenery: spectacular, painfully beautiful, here and there pristine. It was scenery, until I entered into it, until I moved at its pace along its canyon lengths, until I knew its rhythms, until, like Twain's riverboat pilot, I could begin to read its text. Now that I know a few things about it, about its last fifty miles, at least (that old homestead where the pear trees still produce perfect, wormless crops in late September; that grotto of overhanging, honeycomb wheels of columnar basalt, where ferns grow out of the rocks and its stays cool even when the Cougar Canyon air hits 110 degrees or higher); now that I know what little I know, I take great comfort in my enormous ignorance. I could spend every remaining day of my life floating these fifty miles of river, walking the shores, exploring the hills and side canyons and flat, sandy bars, and never know more than a shred of all that the river could tell me. Twain's riverboat pilot suffered from its knowledge. Knowing its shoals and sandbars and snags was necessary, but the knowledge brought with it, well, knowledge. And by such knowing, a good deal of the mystery, and the beauty, was gone. Twain was a writer not often wrong, but about this he was surely somewhat mistaken.

My father is of the generation of men who fought and won World War II, a generation that came of age just as human technology made the jump to apparent warp speed. If he remembers as the first miracle of his life the neighbor lady's simple white Frigidaire, he remembers also when airplanes were rare; he remembers battleships and carriers, as well, and the bombs that brought on v-J Day. And so it is that my father, like many of his generation, was a young man—a young father—enamored of the accomplishments of men, of the things they could build with their wits and hands. On those annual two-week forays into the mountains of Colorado or the hills of Kentucky or Tennessee, we invariably drove, often many miles out of our way, to visit some new dam. I think the idea of it, the fact that someone, somewhere, knew where to start, how to do it: how to block the flow of an entire river! You could have knocked him over with a kiss. He would exclaim and praise, and no doubt we, his children, were suitably impressed. A dam is an awesome, even an awful, thing to behold, to enter, as we often did. I remember feeling the thrum of turbines purling up through the concrete and being aware of the terrible power there. There was nothing mankind could not accomplish in those days, nothing American know-how could not improve upon. To believe so is hubris, of course, the fuel that fires tragedy. It is a little-known fact that the U.S. Army Corps of Engineers (Ed Abbey called them "khaki-shirted little beavers") has plans for dozens of dams along the forks of the Salmon River, should anyone ask them to start building again.

What Huck Finn loved so much about the river was the escape it provided him—from the stultifying dullness of ordinary life, as well as from the awful horror of human hypocrisy. Huck thought of himself as essentially worthless, of low birth and inclined by blood and temperament toward laziness. He loved to loaf. He was in awe of the grand power and status of the steamboat pilot, and he saw only too late the terrible lie behind the barbaric gentility of the Grangerfords and Shepherdsons. When he escaped again and again to the river with Jim, they were borne, ironically, ever deeper into slave country, even as Huck was hauled ever deeper into his own soul.

Here at the mouth of the Salmon River, as elsewhere along its length, the sweet lull of its music hypnotizes. It encourages indolence; it can sing you to sleep. I have spent long, lovely minutes awake and dreaming inside its melody; inside the reach of its spell. Once, way up the South Fork—above the Secesh, above

where the East Fork comes in from over toward Yellow Pine and
Stibnite—I saw a spawned-out chinook salmon floating in a back
eddy pool. I knew, with absolute certainty, that it had come
hundreds of arduous miles from the Pacific Ocean, past the gillnets
and the hungry seals and the dams. I wanted to honor it there, to
say a few words over it—eulogy, poem, or prayer. But as quickly as
words occurred to me, they fattened up, clumsy and maudlin.
Anything I said, I understood, I said for me. Never write a poem,
the poet Dick Hugo advised, about something that ought to
have a poem written about it. I remember I felt foolish, but still I
couldn't bring myself to walk on, so I found a comfortable rock and
sat and sipped from my canteen and ate an apple. Afterward I lay
out across the rock and fell asleep, or at least I think I did; I
might have.

Likely, it was the sound of the water that brought on the vision, if
that's what it was. I was one long muscle. I was swimming, unburdened
by extraneous bones, freed of my cumbersome appendages, my
legs and arms. I could hardly see, such was the speed at
which I moved. By my merest flex and flash, a dazzle of rock shot
by below. There were clouds of froth and clouds beyond the
froth. The light was blue-green and bottomless above me. It was
not so much that I entered the new, blue water, but that it entered
me, a perfect ice in my brain. I was on fire with it, rushing,
going back through what I'd been to what I had to be. Sweet sun
and Jesus river, I leaped, to see the light or clear a stone,
I do not know. My skin glistened; it took my breath away, until
I entered again the froth and current, a froth myself, a splash and
a myth.

That was long ago. I am at the mouth of the river now. My legs, so
long crossed beneath me, tingle, bloodless. This is how it goes,
vision or half-vision in the sound of mountain water. Something
startled me. I'd been staring at the water, or at the sand, or at the
air itself, when I heard it—a stone rolling over in its bed, a fish.
And now I look up and let the light come back, then find
my pencil where it has fallen, and begin to write what the river
says to me.

To be honest, I hope that ruined shoulder of mine is an even less macho, ego-driven enterprise than it might seem. That is to say, I was fairly sure I could throw a rock across the river at Billy Creek, before I even picked one up, but as I have done all my life, I made a silent wager with myself: if I made it, it meant something real; it meant something that mattered to me far beyond distance and arc and muscle. I remember this particular instance perfectly. The rocks I threw that day might as well have been petals from some mopish lovelorn's daisy. She loves me not, she loves me not, she loves me not. Pert near, my grandmother used to say, but not plum.

Of course, what I wanted was to believe in love myself, or to believe in myself as someone capable of and worthy of love. It has just this moment dawned on me, as I think about the river and the times I've spent on it and near it and in it: I have become who I am near rivers, and if I never really loved the Mississippi, it was because I could never give myself over to her entirely. Entering a river requires abandon and luck and faith. It can kill you as easily as a lover can break your heart.

Fool for love that I was, and hope to always be, I found myself that perfect, unimprovable stone, river-round, of the heft of half a baseball. I remember I kissed it, and my cohort thrower laughed. I must have closed my eyes then and come near to meditating; I would have tried to let all the power in my body swirl up from my right leg on a fierce, quick trajectory through my arm. I know I groaned when I let the rock fly. There was a tiny explosion between my collarbone and scapula, a harsh rose of pain, but I knew, when I saw that rock take to the late afternoon air, that this one would make it all the way. And when it hit and bounced among the stones on the opposite shore—clack-clack—I remember I nodded, and smiled, and walked straight on into the cold, welcoming water.

Contributors Notes

HORACE AXTELL AND MARGO ARAGON first met in 1992 when she interviewed him for her award-winning video documentary, *Nee-mee-poo: The Power of Our Dance*. Their collaborative book is entitled *A Little Bit of Wisdom: Conversations with a Nez Perce Elder*. Margo earned her undergraduate degree in English from Lewis-Clark State College and her M.F.A. in Creative Writing from Bennington College in Vermont. Both she and Horace are dedicated to the preservation of Nez Perce language and culture. In addition to studying the language, Margo hosts a bilingual television talk show. Horace lectures all over the world and has twice been one of the subjects of documentary films produced by the British Broadcasting Corporation. He teaches Nez Perce language at Lewis-Clark State College and assists with the Nez Perce Tribal Wolf Education and Research Center.

KIM BARNES lives with her husband and children in the canyon of the Clearwater River. Her memoir about growing up in the timberlands of northern Idaho, *In the Wilderness: Coming of Age in Unknown Country* (Doubleday/Anchor), was a finalist for the 1997 Pulitzer Prize. *Hungry for the World*, her second memoir, was published by Villard in 2000. She teaches creative writing at the University of Idaho in Moscow.

CLAIRE DAVIS received her M.F.A. in fiction at the University of Montana in Missoula, and teaches fiction and literature at Lewis-Clark State College in Lewiston, Idaho. Her short stories have been published in numerous literary magazines, among them: *Southern Review, Shenandoah,* and *Gettysburg Review.* Her short story "Grounded" was included in the *Pushcart Anthology* XXII. In 1998, she received an Idaho Commission on the Arts Fellowship in literature. Her first novel, *Winter Range,* was published by Picador Press in 2000. She is now working on a new collection of short stories.

LOUISE FREEMAN-TOOLE's "Waiting for Coyote" is an excerpt from *Standing up to the Rock: Essays on a Snake River Ranch,* which won the 1998 James L. Fisher Outstanding Thesis Award at Illinois State University and which will be published by the University of Nebraska Press in 2001. After three years in the Midwest, Louise Freeman-Toole and her family have recently returned to the Palouse region on the Washington/Idaho border.

GARY GILDNER's eighteen published books include *Blue Like the Heavens: New & Selected Poems, The Second Bridge* (a novel), *A Week in South Dakota* (short stories), *The Warsaw Sparks* (a memoir about coaching a baseball team in Communist Poland), and *The Bunker in the Parsley Fields,* which received the 1996 Iowa Poetry Prize. He has also received the National Magazine Award for Fiction, A Pushcart Prize, the Robert Frost Fellowship, and the William Carlos Williams and Theodore Roethke poetry prizes. Mr. Gildner has been writer-in-residence at Reed College, Davidson College, and Michigan State University, and a Senior Fulbright Lecturer to Poland and to Czechoslovakia. He has given readings of his work at the Library of Congress, the Academy of American Poets, YM-YWHA (New York), Manhattan Theatre Club, and at some three hundred colleges and schools in the U.S. and abroad.

GUY HAND, a third-generation Idahoan, was born in Twin Falls, raised in Boise, and currently lives in coastal California. He is a freelance writer and radio producer who has written for *Audubon, DoubleTake, High Country News, Northern Lights, Orion,* and

Sierra magazines. He has also produced radio shows for NPR's *Living On Earth* and *The Infinite Mind*.

DEBRA HIERONYMUS completed her M.F.A. degree in Creative Writing at the University of Idaho. She lives just outside Tallahassee, Florida, with her husband, John, her dogs, Bear and Scout, her cat, Gladys, and a canary named Solomon. Her daughter, Judey, attends the University of Idaho.

WILLIAM JOHNSON was born in Portland, Oregon, grew up in Washington and Idaho, taught in New York and Florida, and returned with his family in 1981 to make a permanent home in Idaho. He is a fly-fisherman, a Thoreau scholar, and a poet. His *What Thoreau Said*, a critical reading of *Walden*, appeared in 1991, and a chapbook of poems, *At the Wilderness Boundary*, in 1996. A book-length collection of his poems, *Out of the Ruins*, appeared from Confluence Press in 1999. He was appointed Idaho-Writer-in-Residence for 1998–2001.

LESLIE LEEK is an Idaho native. She grew up in McCammon and Dubois where her family published the *Bannock County News* and the *Clark County Enterprise*, weekly newspapers that, like most, have disappeared. In 1998 she won the *Willow Springs* fiction prize. She currently teaches in the communication and theatre department at Idaho State University in Pocatello.

LESA LUDERS now lives in Lubbock, Texas. She has had stories published in *Willow Springs, Permafrost, Frontiers,* and *A Room of One's Own,* among others. Her novel, *Lady God,* was recently published by New Victoria Press. Currently she is working on a memoir.

RON MCFARLAND has an affinity for rivers, having been born on the Ohio and grown up in Florida between the Indian River and the St. Johns. When he is not fishing the lakes and streams of Idaho, where he has lived since 1970, he teaches seventeenth-century and modern poetry, contemporary Northwest writers, and creative writing at the University of Idaho, where he has served as director of creative writing. He is also an avid soccer player. He is the author of two critical studies, *The World of David Wagoner* (University of Idaho Press, 1997), and *Understanding James Welch* (University of South Carolina Press, 1999). His most recent book of poems is *The Haunting Familiarity of Things* (Singular Speech Press, 1993).

LANCE OLSEN, former Idaho Writer-in-Residence, has written more than a dozen books of or about postmodern fiction, including the novels *Burnt* and *Time Famine*. He teaches creative writing and contemporary fiction at the University of Idaho, and lives with his wife, the artist Andi Olsen, near New Meadows, Idaho. His digital avatar resides at <www.uidaho.edu/~lolsen>.

JOY PASSANANTE teaches literature and creative writing at the University of Idaho. Her essays, stories, and poems have appeared in magazines and journals such as *College English, Short Story, Xavier Review*, and *Talking River Review*. Her collection of poems, *Sinning in Italy*, was published by Limberlost Press in 1999. A novel, *My Mother's Lovers*, is forthcoming from the University of Nevada Press in 2001.

DIANE JOSEPHY PEAVEY lives on a sheep and cattle ranch in south central Idaho. She writes stories about that life and the changing landscape of the West that are aired weekly on Idaho Public Radio. Her work has appeared in numerous magazines and journals including *Boise* magazine, *The Cabin, Talking River Review, Range* magazine, *Imprint, Northern Lights*, and the anthologies *Shadow Cat* (Sasquatch Press, 1999), *Where the Morning Light's Still Blue* (University of Idaho Press, 1994), and *Woven on the Wind* (Houghton Mifflin), forthcoming in 2001. Fulcrum Press will publish a collection of her essays in 2001.

JOHN REMBER was born in the Sun Valley Lodge in 1950, and was raised in Sawtooth Valley, where his father was a fishing guide and fur trapper and his mother was a nurse. He was awarded an M.F.A. from the University of Montana in 1987. He teaches at Albertson College.

WILLIAM STUDEBAKER was born in Salmon, Idaho, to post-pioneer parents who kept the family wandering among the mountains of central Idaho. He attended Salmon public schools, Idaho State University, and the University of Idaho, studying history, English, law, and mythology. Since settling near Twin Falls in the 1970s, he has taught at the College of Southern Idaho. His latest books are *River Religion* (Limberlost Press, 1997), *Travelers in an Antique Land* (University of Idaho Press, 1997), *Short of a Good Promise* (Washington State University Press, 1999), and *Little Lenny's Christmas*, forthcoming from Limberlost Press. He is passionate about dogs, landscape, private relationships, and rivers.

JULIE TITONE grew up amid the Midwest's cornfields and muddy reservoirs and graduated from Southern Illinois University with a journalism degree. She drove west to join the staff of *The Idaho Statesman* in 1974, where she worked as a reporter and then an editor. In 1975, she was astonished by her first sight of a raging western river, the North Fork of the Payette. She has been at *The Spokesman-Review* since 1985, working alternately in its Spokane and Coeur d'Alene offices as editor and reporter. Her work also has appeared in such publications as *The New York Times, American Forests, American Medical News,* and *California Wild!;* in *Where the Morning Light's Still Blue,* a book of Idaho essays; and in *Reading the Environment,* a college text.

ROBERT WRIGLEY has published five books of poetry, the most recent of which is *Reign of Snakes* (Penguin Books, 1999). A former Guggenheim Fellow, as well as a two-time NEA Fellow, he lives with his family in Lenore, Idaho.

AGMV Marquis

MEMBER OF THE SCABRINI GROUP

Quebec, Canada
2001